Under the Table

Drinking Games to Liven Up Your Parties

Scott Tharler

D1379046

PRC

Produced in 2003 by
PRC Publishing Limited,
The Chrysalis Building
Bramley Road, London W10 6SP
An imprint of **Chrysalis** Books Group plc

This edition published in 2003
Distributed in the U.S. and Canada by:
Sterling Publishing Co., Inc.
387 Park Avenue South
New York, NY 10016

ISBN 1 85648 659-1

Printed and bound in Malaysia

All illustrations by Robyn Neild
(© PRC Publishing Limited).

Caution: Drinking distilled spirits, beers, coolers,
wine, and other alcoholic beverages may increase
cancer risk and during pregnancy can cause birth defects.

Under the Table

Contents

Acknowledgments

The dynamic and perplexing world of drinking games is filled with kooky conundrums. For example, the people with the most empirical gaming experience, by definition, tend to wind up with the most beer-bludgeoned brains. And yet, without the guidance of such often memory-challenged benefactors, assembling this fine compendium would not have been possible.

Thanks to my Kappa Delta Rho brothers (Barry Wood, Chris Kaczmarek, Joe Nesteriak and his lovely wife Kyra, Peter Weingarten, Mike "Spanky" Godofsky, Zach Miller, Mike "Taco" Belle, Jim Dispenza, Dave Coxhead, Eric Fleischer, Jon Eskenas, Jon Lay, Rafi Isaac, and P. Andrew Leynes), my other fellow Syracuse University alumni (Kate Donovan, Alaina Smith, Jason Cohen, Steve Bradbury, Siani Kiyonaga, Regie Belen, Russell Ford, Stan Dlugozima, Fred L. Russell, Anthony J. Salemi, Trevor Dellecave, Mike and Wil Fox) and all the other research-friendly friends and family who helped the various rules and nuances to come flooding back (Tad Stewart, Liz Foster, Vicki Anderson, P. Andrew Bilbao, David Bromley, Jim O'Donnell, Jen Tharler, Jack Edmonston, Norma Cancellari, Sarah Eadie, Sai Man, Joe D'Eramo, Leslie Dondero, Carrie Miller, Becky Lansky, Jennifer Lansky, Richard Lansky, David Isaac, Todd Winnick, Jay Lerner, Jennifer Paez, Marc Nobleman, Michael Garber, Josh Weissman, and Mick Kelly).

Finally, very special thanks to these dear souls for repeatedly providing their invaluable inspiration and advice: Doug Lansky, Bruce Lansky, and Louise Lansky; loving grandparents David and Sara Lansky and Stanley and Muriel Tharler; and my ever-supportive parents, Elaine Lansky and Steven Tharler. They're the ones who really deserve a drink!

Preface

This light-hearted guide is by all means designed expressly for your entertainment. But it in no way condones or encourages alcohol abuse—especially underage drinking, binge drinking, or driving while under the influence. So please use your head throughout all the free-spirited merriment. Do your best to preserve the delicate balance between a good time and something that would make Ted Kennedy blush. Know your physical limitations and when to quit. And most importantly, obey the laws in your community and look out for the health and safety of those around you. Excessive drinking can cause irreparable harm to your own body and jeopardize others. If you feel you or a friend has a problem, you may want to contact Alcoholics Anonymous (www.aa.org)—or just try playing any of the games as described, but substitute your favorite nonalcoholic drink. Most of the games are cool enough that you could still be social and have a good time without the booze.

Introduction

The very nature of drinking games embodies enigmas that have riddled "partiers" for generations. At the inner core is the fact that in social situations, where the act of drinking would appear to be the main endeavor, having to actually imbibe is generally the big penalty, the thing to avoid. Of course, at some point you definitely will want to avoid drinking. Because, ironically, said drinking penalties perpetually make it trickier to follow the rules and play these alco-frolicky activities properly. In other words, the more mistakes, the more booze; the more booze, the more mistakes; and so goes the sickly cycle. If that's how it's going to be, you might ask yourself, why bother with these crazy diversions in the first place? Why not just drink?

First off, it doesn't take long for plain drinking to become downright boring. Second, and more importantly, most people enjoy any opportunity for competition. It gives them a chance to flaunt their superiority. And nothing feels better than besting your buddies with sharp verbal acuity, trivial knowledge, coin-bouncing, or card-playing skills—or even just knowing how to play the games in the first place.

Pretty much any activity can be turned into a drinking game, from sitting on the porch and noting the various colors of cars passing by, to playing classic board games, to mindlessly watching TV. Obviously, more heated disputes tend to arise from the more complicated games that have several variations. But that's all the more reason for all the players to understand the rules and establish a fair procedure for dealing with any discrepancies during play (such as by a majority vote of hands). If this book helps to ward off just one of those inevitably inebriated idiots who likes to make up games as they go, this book will have served its sacred purpose.

How to Use This Book

The Sections: They have been intentionally organized to benefit newbies as well as...well, oldbies. Whichever you be, it doesn't matter where you start. It's not meant to be read cover to cover like a novel—even though the prose sparkles like that of any Clancy, Poe, or Hemingway. So jump around section to section. Whatever game you wind up at will be juxtaposed by ones with a similar M.O., rather than just having in common that they use cards or dice. Certain games may seem like they fit (better) in another section. True, but just know that the overall grouping was done in a way that attempted to make logical sense.

The Descriptions: The game write-ups have been laid out in a way that gives the basic concepts and gets you right into playing as quickly as possible. The idea being that your goal may be hardcore sociological research, but, more likely, just to play the games! Speaking of which, whoever comes up with the idea of what to play generally gets to start the game or be the dealer: whichever's more advantageous.

Where applicable, the most popular aliases and other rules and variations are listed in parentheses. So if someone at a house party shouts, "Hey, how about Libya?" you can quickly surmise that they're talking probably about a special brand of the Beer Pong game Beirut, not foreign affairs. Because they are so popular and have so many rules, many games, like Kings for instance, have the potential for tons of bastardized versions. Try to be patient with miscreants who don't know how to play the "real" way as listed here. Who knows? You might find cooler ways to play. But probably not. If they were really cooler, they'd already be listed here.

The Rituals: To be sure, drinking games engender more than just the rules on each description page. Surrounding every game is a universe of (until now) untapped, unwritten rules of etiquette. Knowing these rituals will help you to understand when to act and how to respond appropriately to various verbal and nonverbal cues. Sounds kind of like a behavioral psychology experiment. Well, in a way, it is! And the aversional zap you'll feel will be all your friends (or, worse yet, strangers) laughing at you while you have to drink. To avoid this socially scarring situation, it's definitely a good idea—if you can display the patience of a champion—to peruse each of the five rituals discussed throughout before you jump into the actual games.

Winning Your Next Drink: As stated in the Introduction (if you took the time to read it), much of the essence of drinking games has to do with the sport of it all. The competition, pitting wit against wit and skill against skill. In that spirit, this book displays a decathlon of direct challenges. Several of the finest bar bets around. In between games, they'll help you to triumph over whatever poor challengee you choose to make look foolish—and better yet, owe you your next drink! On a closing self-congratulatory note, you'll find that each of the bets befits the category of the section they follow. In other words, a bet about movie stars follows the section on entertainment media, one involving great coordination follows the section on skills, and one for even the most simple-minded sap follows the section called Dumb Luck.

The Appendices: They're mostly just hints on how to spice up the games you like and create new ones on your own. You might want to glance at them a little bit during play, but don't bust your hump memorizing them or anything. They're just little ways to make you a more worldly player. So it's probably better to check them out before or after actual gameplay.

In General: Unless otherwise specified, it's usually a good idea to utilize beer as your spirit of choice. Except if you have the tolerance of a Russian premier and the hard stuff just happens to be your thing. Either way, any of the penalty assessments mentioned are somewhat arbitrary and can by all means be adjusted to whatever's comfortable for you.

Along similar lines, these particular drinking games were selected because most of them are cool games. Ones you might even play (heaven forbid) without the alcohol. On the contrary, a few of them are so ridiculous that you might need alcohol to make them tolerable. By the way, just in case you're curious, you won't find info in here about how to do an invert, kill a keg, or any other "power drinking" methods. Because although they do involve drinking and might be sporting enough to be considered games, they're mostly just about mindless mass consumption and not very interesting to write about!

Through experimentation you'll find that certain games are better played in particular settings. Fast action games like Quarters and Catch the Pig that tend to require a beer rag are best played in a bar where you don't care about unavoidable spillage. The game Sex, Drugs, and Rock 'n' Roll, where you actually need to be able to hear the person in order to respond, is best played at a relatively quiet house party where there are fewer people and less distractions.

Lastly, a quick word about the gender bias throughout the book. Whenever referring to players, I use "he" or "his" because I'm basically placing myself (a male) in the role of the player. It's not to imply that any of these pleasurable diversions aren't fine games for any women who knowingly choose to engage in them. It should go without saying that the ultimate goal of this book is for anyone and everyone who reads it to find some way (hopefully multiple ways) to have fun. So go for it. Cheers, and good luck!

The Ritual of Giving and Taking Drinks

In verbal contests like those in Section 3, if you hesitate in giving a response, you'll be expected to "drink while you think." It's a bitch, but that's what happens when you waste everyone's happy fun time. That's one example of a penalty, which means you consume as punishment for violating a rule during gameplay.

This is opposed to a "party foul," which means you've screwed up on a different level. You might have thrown "sloppy dice," meaning they rolled right off the table—although the term can be applied to any careless act involving game props, such as the spilling of alcohol. God save you if that happens. Players tend to frown on this form of "alcohol abuse."

It's generally accepted that, especially for larger infractions, whenever doling out (versus facing) a penalty, you can split the punishment between any number of players. The piper may be paid in drinks (little gulps), seconds (counted by yourself or another player), or fingers (a representation using the height of the digits wrapping around your cup/bottle to indicate how much beverage needs to disappear).

How much is "a drink?" Unfortunately, because of the different measurement systems above and the fact that different people are motivated to take in more or less each time, there's really no clear-cut, scientific answer. Having said that, setting boundaries is smart. For example, you might want to establish early on that ten sips equals half a beer and twenty a full one. Or whatever seems fair, based on the types of games you'll be playing and general consensus.

Bluffing: Generally not a good idea. Someone is likely to figure your clever ruse when they notice you've been nursing the same twelve-ouncer through three rounds of Up and Down the River. If you do drink a bit short each time, at least make sure you're sipping from a can. Our opaque little pal will make it trickier to see that not much is going down your gullet.

Conversely, if you're handing out a punishment and your victim finishes their beer before you're done counting, that puts the burden on you. Especially if a lot is owed at one time, ask how much they have left before any beer touches their lips. Depending on how you're feeling, you can either tell them to just kill what they've got or kill it and take a drag off their new drink as well. If you don't specify anything (and they're aware of your faux pas), you can be made to complete their sentence.

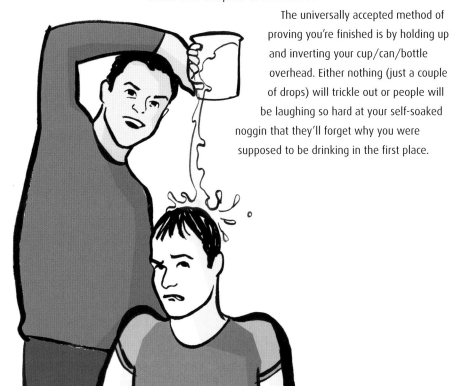

The universally accepted method of proving you're finished is by holding up and inverting your cup/can/bottle overhead. Either nothing (just a couple of drops) will trickle out or people will be laughing so hard at your self-soaked noggin that they'll forget why you were supposed to be drinking in the first place.

SECTION 1: Ten Classics Every Gamer Should Know

Originating in ancient Babylonia and popularized by the Carthaginians, these classic games are proudly played to this day in many Amish communities. These are highly celebrated hall-of-famers that'll serve as boot camp for beginners and a refresher for not-so-neophytes.

Spoons

- Required: Between three and thirteen players, some cards, and enough spoons for all but one of the players.
- Summary: A fast-paced game of trading cards and grabbing at objects to avoid being the odd man out.

Playing: Pull as many collections of four of a kind from the deck as you have players at the table. (It doesn't matter if it's all the aces, fours, tens, etc.) Place the spoons equidistant from all the players. Shuffle and deal out the cards. Everyone waits to pick up their cards at the same time, at which point the dealer yells, "Pass [to the left]!" and each player passes a single card [to the left]. Good dealers don't wait more than a few seconds to shout "Pass!" again, sometimes switching the direction and never letting anyone get too comfortable with their cards. Your mission in the mayhem is to get four of any kind you can without ripping the cards or losing any digits. The first person to do so calmly puts down their cards and grasps a spoon. Every other player observing this immediately tries to nab one (regardless of their card situation). Sammy Slow-on-the-Draw must drink for his sloth-like reflexes and patiently watch from the sidelines as additional rounds are played (each time removing another spoon and foursome of cards).

Other Rules and Variations

- Relate the drinking to the value of the four of a kind, the number of people left, or just some arbitrary amount.
- Decide ahead of time whether full possession of the spoon or just grabbing the big end wins. If it's the former, be prepared to be dragged all over the room, if necessary.
- If the initiator of the spoon melee is found not to have had a proper four-of-a-kind, they must finish whatever they're drinking.

Mexican (a.k.a. Mexicali, Mex, Liar's Dice)

- Required: A cup, a pair of dice, a pair of cajones, and two to four hombres.
- Summary: Roll dem bones until you can either beat the previous roll or fool others into thinking you did.

Playing: Roller number one has up to three chances to get what he considers a decent score. From best to worst, the rolls go:

2:1, 6:6, 5:5, 4:4, 3:3, 2:2, 1:1, 6:5, 6:4, 6:3, 6:2,
6:1, 5:4, 5:3, 5:2, 5:1, 4:3, 4:2, 4:1, 3:2, 3:1

Players only get as many rolls as the round's first roller took to beat his score. When the dice fail to cooperate is when you need to lie like a politician. Hence the cup. Use it to hide each roll and fib when necessary. When challenged, show the challenger whether you're lying (or not) and (have them) drink accordingly. Other times to drink include when you've thrown the lowest score of the round and a compulsory for everyone anytime a "4:1" appears. Throwing a "2:1"—or "Mexican"—is the greatest possible achievement in the game and allows the player to dole out a drink on the spot. By the way, notice that in the fourteen non-doubles rolls the higher number is always listed first (since it gives you a higher score). Drink if you call something non-existent ("1:6" or "3:5" or "2:4") that foolishly cheats yourself!

Other Rules and Variations

- The penalty for being worst in a round doubles for each Mexican thrown that round.
- On the first or second turn, overly optimistic players can hold either a 1 or 2 for one roll; but if they don't get the complementary 2 or 1 for a Mexican, they can't re-roll the same die again.
- Ties for a low score can be settled by three tosses.
- Naturally, anyone who rolls either die off the table or loses a die should pay a stiff penalty!

Kings (a.k.a. California Kings, Queens, King's Court)

- Required: Four or more nobles with brew-filled flagons, one large glass, and a deck of cards.
- Summary: Every card turned over symbolizes a pre-determined action that needs to be performed.

Playing: The cards are spread out upside down in a big circle around the large glass. Players turn over one card at a time with the following consequences:

Ace: Everyone drinks.

Two through four: If it's black, take that many sips; if it's red, give that many sips.

Five: The Thumb. Whoever's last to put one on the table drinks.

Six: Skips to the next person.

Seven: The person to your left drinks.

Eight: The person across from you drinks.

Nine: The person to your right drinks.

Ten: Categories. Make up any topic and go around the table until someone fails to blurt out an appropriate item for that category...and has to drink.

Jack: The men drink. (A toast may be in order.)

Queen: The women drink. (A toast is definitely in order!)

King: Those who reveal each of the first three kings fill the large glass in the center of the table with however much of their beer as they want. The flipper of the fourth king has to finish off the glass!

Other Rules and Variations

Face-up cards go in the discard pile and aren't used again in the round. Anyone who's supposed to drink and is too slow drinks double. For the categories, the more specific ("Car Models That Begin With the Letter T," " Museums," "Ozzy Osbourne Songs," "European Beers," "Four-Legged Animals," "Cigarette Brands," "Cartoon Dogs," "Sexual Positions") the better the challenge. Also feel free to use fewer cards, swap in any rules (such as the ones found in Appendix B) or quickies (such as can be found in The Ritual of Combining Games, just before Section 9), if you like. A few common ones to try:

- Aces initiate categories and tens start a Social.
- Low cards (two to four) equal taking that many drinks and medium cards (five to eight) equal giving that many drinks.
- A particular card means the last person to touch their nose has to drink.
- People take turns saying words that rhyme with the last word in a sentence you say.
- No one goes to the bathroom until another of the card just turned shows up again.
- Get out of drinking free card. (If three kings are turned, save it for the end!)
- Forget the glass in the middle and its potential for awful concoctions. Each player who turns over a king starts a Waterfall (see The Ritual of Continuous Consumption).

Thumper

- Required: A bunch of silly people sitting in a circle.
- Summary: The granddaddy of all goofy gesturing/tag games.

Playing: Each person shows the group the gesture they want to be known by for the game. It can incorporate the hands, arms, face, sound, movement—whatever, as long as it's creative and somewhat memorable. Once everyone's chosen their gesture, it's a good idea to go around the circle displaying each of them as a reminder for everyone. (Including yourself—nothing's more embarrassing and punishable than forgetting your own sign!) Then the drumming starts. With everyone rhythmically pounding on the table, the leader (usually whoever brought up the idea to play) bellows, "What is the name of the game?" Everyone replies "Thumper!" Leader: "Why do we play it?" Group: "To get wrecked!" The leader then does his gesture, followed by another player's. Whoever's gesture it is responds by doing his gesture and another's. And so it continues, with anyone who isn't gesturing continuing to drum and whoever breaks the cycle drinking. It's hard to imagine an atmosphere where this sort of freakish behavior wouldn't stand out. So if this game is your cup of tea, you shouldn't have a problem finding folks playing. Obviously, the more players you have, the trickier it is.

Variations: With such a popular granddaddy, you're bound to get at least a couple of trashy cousins. Certain crass individuals have seen fit to create vulgar variations on this theme. Use your imagination. If this eccentric form of expression is your bag, see Section 3.

Three Man

- Required: A pair of dice and two to five thirsty three-minded people.
- Summary: If you're the Three Man, hope a three doesn't come up!

Playing: Players take turns rolling a single die. The first one to roll a three is the lucky Three Man. It's his job to drink whenever a three comes up, in total or on either die. Statistically, that's a thirteen in thirty-six chance, or only about thirty-six percent of the time; but it always seems like so much more when you're the Three Man! When the Three Man finally rolls another three, he may transfer his honorable trifectorial duties to the poor, unfortunate soul of his choice.

Throwing doubles precipitates a Punishment Round. The dice are given to another player or split between two players and rolled. If different numbers come up on the two dice, that many sips must be taken by the roller(s); if (even split) doubles appear, the punishment boomerangs back to the original roller, who must drink the total and continue his turn.

Naturally, if a three comes up in the Punishment Round, the Three Man is still obligated to imbibe. If three consecutive doubles are rolled in regular play, that player can—depending on how you want to play—earn the privilege of either making up a rule or (quite contrarily) becoming the new Three Man. As you can imagine, when double threes are rolled, bedlam ensues. Finally, in the off chance that someone rolls something not requiring drinking, their turn is over and they pass the dice.

Other Rules and Variations

Much like the game Kings, if the action gets too slow, you can assign various drinking duties to different totals. Just keep in mind that these extra little celebrations will lengthen each player's turn—but with more drinking, you may not care if you're the one rolling the dice. Typical responses to totals rolled are:

- Five: Last person with a thumb on the table drinks (keeping in mind that the Three Man has to drink on 3:2 rolls anyway).
- Seven: Player to the left drinks.
- Nine: Player to the right drinks.
- Eleven: Everyone drinks.

Fives, a similarly numerical dice game, can, by coincidence, be found in Section 5.

Sweeper (a.k.a President)

- **Required: Cards and four to six humble-able authority-seekers.**
- **Summary: The skill of bridge combined with the potential for teeter-tottering egomaniacal power struggles. Avoid the bedspin-inducing title role by not getting rid of your cards last in each round.**

Playing: Shuffle the cards and deal them clockwise (a few at a time to speed things up) until the pack is spent. In the spirit of the game, those who didn't step up to deal this first round should really drink for not volunteering. For this initial "qualifying" round, the person to the left of the dealer makes the first play.

Usually this will be a low card, since i) each successive card played must be of higher value than the one just played, and ii) it becomes increasingly difficult to ditch the junk in your hand as the game progresses. The crummiest cards are threes; followed by fours through kings; then aces; and finally twos, which kick ass. If it's your turn and you can't or don't want to play a higher card—and it must be higher, not equal—then you pass by taking a sip of beer. When the passing and sipping goes all the way around to the person who played the last card, the cards are swept and that person leads next.

> **Side note:** Things tend to move along much faster when folks can play their multiples (two, three, or four of a kind) at any point in the round. But once doubles are played, either higher doubles or any triples or quads must follow. For instance, if someone plays a king, you could put double threes on that, your neighbor could dish double eights on that and their neighbor could throw triple fives on that. More cards always beat fewer cards. And a (single) two beats everything. Whenever the deuce is played, the cards are swept and whoever dropped the two-bomb immediately leads next.

Play continues until the first crafty soul to be without cards shouts, "President!" The next players to go out successively yell, "Vice [President]!" and then, "Treasurer!" and then, "Secretary!" and finally, "Cool, I'm not Sweeper!" (Naturally, depending on the number of

23

players, there may be more or less such yellers.) At that point, all eyes turn to the new Sweeper and the laughing begins. That's because the responsibilities of the Sweeper include: Shuffling, dealing, sweeping the cards, and drinking at the request of anyone at any time for any reason (since he is outranked by everyone playing). Especially for screwing up dealing or sweeping the cards, but often for no good reason whatsoever.

Conversely, the incoming President gets to choose which seat he wants (whereupon everyone else shifts to sit in order of decreasing rank, starting in whatever direction the big cheese wishes), can obviously tell anyone to drink and has other privileges. Such as the singular ability to begin a round by calling a "Board Meeting." Basically (just as with a "Waterfall," as described in The Ritual of Continuous Consumption), everyone stands, starts drinking at the same time, and can't stop until the person directly above them in rank does! As if that weren't enough, the Sweeper must deal in such a way (starting with himself and proceeding away from the President) to ensure that more cards fill the hands of the low-rankers. Plus, he must then give the President his best card (usually a two) in exchange for the President's trashiest card (usually a three or four).

Believe it or not, despite the obvious built-in impediments to upward mobility, it is possible for the Sweeper to get out of the basement. But it's rare for him to go all the way to the Penthouse in one round. Still, ranks do tend to change every round, so you may want to be careful on whom you dump. Or better yet, just dump on anyone you can while you have the fleeting chance!

Strategy tip: Hold onto that two for as long as you can! Typically, the way folks go out each round is by playing (multiples and then) a two and leading off the next series with their final, crappiest card. If you don't have a two or a nice set of multiples, going out will be definitely harder.

Other Rules and Variations

· Join a game in progress and you automatically earn a starting position as Sweeper.

· Ring in each round with a toast to the President.

· Allow "re-elected" Presidents to decree wacky rules (see Appendix B), such as that players need to say "fumf" when playing a five.

· Limit playing multiples (two, three, or more of a kind) to leading a round or following such a lead.

· Allow playing cards of equal (not necessarily higher) value, which then skips the next person's turn.

· Everyone drinks when three of the same-valued card are played in the same round—even, for instance, if a single is played earlier and then a double of that same value later in that round.

· If more than seven people play: Add another deck; enlist a Vice Sweeper (second to last to go out in the previous round) to ensure the overworked Sweeper doesn't slow down the game; make the Vice Sweeper and VP exchange one good/bad card and the Sweeper and President now two; require two twos to kill five-or-more-of-a-kind.

For other similarly serious strategic games, see Section 2.

Fizz-Buzz (a.k.a. Bizz-Buzz)

- **Required:** At least a few mathematical geniuses who can count out loud.
- **Summary:** See how high you can get (again, by counting) when substituting special utterances for certain numbers.

6×8 64
63 $9 \times 8 = 72$
70 $10 \times 8 = 80$ 7
$11 \times 8 = 88$

Playing: Starting with "one" (go figure), each player counts off as fast as possible. When a number that's a multiple of five or has a five in it (e.g. five, twenty, fifty-one) comes up, in lieu of naming that number, the player whose turn it is says "Fizz." Likewise, when a number comes up that's a multiple of seven or has a seven in it (e.g. fourteen, twenty-seven, forty-two) the player whose turn it is goes "Buzz." As many of you calculus-crunching theorists may be thinking, "What about numbers like thirty-five or fifty-seven, which are multiples of or contain both five and seven?" For those, a cry of "Fizz-Buzz" will suffice. And yes, if you make it to fifty-five or seventy-seven, a yell of "Fizz-Fizz" or "Buzz-Buzz" is appropriate. But alas, whenever someone hesitates or screws up, they consume and the count starts all over. So don't be disappointed if your group doesn't surpass twenty-seven or so. If it does, you're probably either not going fast enough or aren't (fizz-)buzzed enough.

Other Rules and Variations

· Instead of "Fizz," sub in "Bizz"—or for that matter, any other weird word, sound, or action.
· Don't reset the count unless the mess-up occurs after a certain number. Or perhaps reset the count to one, eleven, twenty-one, thirty-one, etc., so you don't have to keep repeating the same annoying sequence! Better yet, if someone keeps ruining it, make them finish their beer and leave the table.
· If it's a little late in the evening and/or the crowd seems a little slow, try using instances or multiples of seven and eleven (or just seven) as the magic replacement numbers.
· If everyone's a little too fast, step up to the big leagues with Bizz-Buzz-Bang, which uses threes, fives and sevens (i.e. "one," "two," "Bizz," "four," "Buzz," "Bizz," "Bang," "eight," "Bizz," "Buzz," "eleven," etc.)! If the group makes it up to seventy with no problem, you're most likely surrounded by idiot savants and should stop what you're doing and book the next flight you can to Las Vegas.

- If you can count on one thing, it's that Section 5 has a few other games like this.

Beirut (a.k.a Beer Pong, Libya)

· Required: A long table, several cups of beer, and two to six bombardiers.
· Summary: Try to bounce a ping-pong ball into a cup on your opponents' side.

Playing: One way to play is basically just like regular ping-pong, with paddles and everything, except you have a single beer sitting toward each end of the table in the middle (or toward each of the corners if playing doubles). The same basic rule of it-can-only-bounce-once-on-your-side still applies. But since you might not have paddles or an actual regulation table (but still manage to have a ping-pong ball lying around for some strange reason), another way to play is simply by bouncing the ball right from your hand. Either way, hitting your opponent's cup means they take a sip; and if it lands in the cup, they down whatever's left in the cup (save the ball itself) and it's refilled. The ball is in play until it clearly goes off the table. (Germ-conscious players can catch it before the ball hits the ground.) Interfering with a ball in play is strictly forbidden and punishable by a penalty drink. For that and any other agreed-on infractions, you should have a spare beer off the table and within reach.

Other Rules and Variations

· If a cup is knocked over, the player responsible owes a drink and must refill it.
· The order could go you (your partner(s)), your opponent (his partner(s)). Or play that if someone gets one in (rather than just hitting the cup), they get the ball back.
· Especially with more people, it's fun to try it with more cups and different configurations, such as a pyramid, an hourglass, a diamond, etc.
· For these multi-cup versions, you can refill empty cups, remove them and form a new shape or leave the empties up there. If the other team lands in one, they have to drink!

Similar games of skill can be found in Section 4.

Quarters

· **Required: Two or more players with at least one coin and cup.**
· **Summary: Bounce the dirty currency into some clean beer and hope the alcohol kills the bacteria. With a concept so inherently simple, and coinage so readily available, this is pretty much the universal drinking game.**

Playing: Pretty basic. Shooters take turns trying to bounce a quarter off the table and into a glass. (Whoever whips out a quarter first gets first crack at it.) You can experiment with different tables and drinking vessels. But the bigger choice is whether you'll be aiming directly at an opponent's cup or toward a neutral cup—most likely with at least a little liquid in it, to help avoid jaw-droppingly frustrating bounce-outs. The permeating premise throughout is that if you make it into a glass, you get to make someone else at the table drink; if you don't, you get to pass the quarter so someone else can try.

If a player is feeling especially bold, after a miss he can call a "Safety" or "Chance," which gives him an extra shot. If he makes it, play continues as normal. If he misses, the drink penalty at least doubles and he loses his turn. Some folks play so that there's also a penalty for "rimmers," but the telltale clink-and-table-bounce seems like torture enough. Conversely, the reward for a skilled marksman, who makes three in a row, is that they get to make up a rule (see Appendix B).

Other Rules and Variations

Most bouncers use their thumb and index or middle finger, bouncing the face of the quarter. Others use their own face, letting the coin roll down their nose, bounce on its side and into the glass. With whichever method suits you best, here are just a few of the many fun varieties of Quarters:

Chandeliers: Place several smaller glasses around a larger one and fill all of them with beer. If you sink it, they drink it. In the Robo-Slam version, you aim for your own drinks first, which you (believe or not) want to finish fast. Because then you get to move on to the biggie in the middle. Whoever gets the quarter in there makes the other individual or team finish it. If someone gets it in the big'n before finishing their littler drinks, they're sunk...literally.

Speed (a.k.a. Chase): Two shot glasses are placed on opposite sides of a large glass. As players successfully bounce the quarter into one of the shots, they pass the coin/glass in one direction. As soon as someone has both shots in front of them, they're obligated to drink from the monster in the middle. Similarly frantic is Rapid Fire, the ultimate in multiplayer excitement. Any number of players shoots for the same cup. Last one in has to down it—but then presumably has an easier time coming up with laundry money that week.

Skeeball (a.k.a. Evil Kneivel): Three to five vessels are placed in a line going away from the shooter, small to large. When you make it in one of them, you get to make others drink that one and every one smaller than it. (Thus it's best to get it in the largest, farthest cup possible.) If you happen to have an ice-tray lying around, you can play a similar version called Cubes. Place the tray lengthwise (so you're looking at six or seven rows of two). Then when you bounce a quarter into a compartment on the left side, you give the number of drinks corresponding to how many rows it is away from you. But land in the right side and you take that many. And if you land in the farthest row (either side), folks yell "Moose!" The last one to respond properly (see The Ritual of Reacting to Exclamations and Gestures) must take a big ol' sip.

Again, the Quarters franchise aligns best with the games of skill found in Section 4.

Up and Down the River (a.k.a. Up the River, Down the River, Give and Take)

- Required: A deck of cards and anywhere from three to eight people who want to get sloshed.
- Summary: Give or take drinks based on matching cards. When the game's over, you may feel like you were on a whitewater-rafting ride!

Playing: Everyone gets four cards dealt face up in front of them. The dealer then turns over a card from the remaining pile and says, "Take one." People drink one for each card in front of them that matches the turned card. For "Take two," they take two drinks for each card...and so on through "Take four." At that point, it reverses from the "Give four" round on down to "Give one." The sequence can be repeated until the deck is spent—or the players are.

Other Rules and Variations

Try setting up the cards in the middle as a six-row pyramid (one, two, three, four, five, and six cards in each row) or a five-row diamond (two, three, four, three, and two cards in each row). Then deal out the rest of the cards to the player. A card in the first row is flipped. Whoever can match it, discards right onto that card and takes a drink for as many cards as are in that row. You can alternate taking and giving drinks either card-by-card or row-by-row, whichever floats your boat.

For an interesting twist on the ending, see The Ritual of Combining Games. And for similar games, see Across the Bridge, Horse Race, Drunk Driver, and Circle of Death.

How to Win Your Next Drink: The Cup Trick

This is a classic trick to end a classic section.

The Set-up: You'll need three empty cups placed in a row, with the ones on the end pointing down and the middle one in the up position. Leading by example, you tell the mark that the goal is to turn over two cups at a time with two turns and have them all end "up." You flip cups one and two, then two and three and you're done. It seems so simple, they'll look at you like you're an idiot when you bet them they can't do it.

The Trick: When you reverse the necessary set-up for them, by having the end cups up and the middle one down, you'll see who the idiot is! From that start, it's impossible, so just make sure each of their tries begins two up, one down. ★

★ Alternatively, you can start with all three cups in the up position and do the maneuver in three moves. Just make sure that others attempting it start from the all-down position.

SECTION 2: Employing a Little Strategy

This section is for the clever gamer who wants to outwit his friends (or some unsuspecting strangers).

Golf

- Required: Three to five duffers and no clubs or balls, just cards.
- Summary: Shoot for the lowest score (point total) possible.

Playing: Players are each dealt four cards and approach the hole by teeing up two up, two down. The top deck card is turned over to represent the discard pile and placed next to the rest of the pack. The player (to the dealer's left) chooses between that one and a fresh-but-blind one from the top of the deck. If the player keeps either, he discards. Otherwise he just tosses the reject right into the discard pile. Play continues with players choosing from the tops of the rejects or the deck, until one cocky player thinks he has the lowest four-card total and knocks. His turn is literally just rapping the table twice with his knuckles or saying, "Hey fellas, I'm knocking." It goes around one last time to give every other player a chance to improve his score and then the cards are revealed. Aces are worth one, court cards (jacks, queens, and kings) are zero and the rest are their face value. If no one can beat the player who knocked, the losers each drink their totals. If someone either beats or ties him, he drinks double his total. Obviously, the tricky part is that players don't know their down cards until they replace them. As you can imagine, nothing's worse than swapping in a tasty-looking trey (three) and having to swap out a stone-cold king (zero). But that's the chance you take when you play the fair way (sorry!). In any case, nine holes (rounds) is probably a fine outing for most folks, unless you have the skill and stamina of a John Daly.

Strategy tips: Sub out your down cards as soon as possible, but not with values higher than four—unless it's the last pass and you're trying to cut your losses. Speaking of which, don't even think about knocking with a known total higher than six (especially the more people playing), unless it's in the first or second pass, you have two or less points showing and you hope to get lucky and catch everyone off guard.

Other Rules and Variations

- If hackers need a handicap, allow them the luxury of glancing at their two down cards at the beginning of each hole. It strains the brain slightly less and makes it more a game of luck and bluffing. But most likely, after a few trips around the table folks will forget what they have anyway. At which point you can enforce a penalty drink for the privilege of letting them have an extra peek.
- Instead of straight sips based on each loser's total, another method of punishment is for the round's winner to count as the losers simultaneously drink until the difference between the winner's total and theirs is reached.

If you like this one, Screw Your Neighbor, later in this section, has a similar lower-cards-are-better theme.

Gauntlet (a.k.a. Card Sharks—after the 1978 game show where actress Markie Post got her first TV break as a giant-card-turning model.)

- Required: A deck of cards and two brave knights.
- Summary: Make your way through a series of cards based on successfully guessing high or low.

Playing: The dealer creates the gauntlet by setting two rows of seven cards face-down. Starting with the leftmost column, a card from the top row is turned up and the player guesses whether the card in the bottom row will be higher or lower. An incorrect estimation results in penalty drinking. Matching two like-valued cards in the same column doubles the penalty. There's a reason it's called "the gauntlet" and not "the cakewalk!" In any case, the guess moves to the next column and the prediction process repeats. The player who survives the trip across the gauntlet without any mistakes is crowned dealer and the roles reverse.

Other Rules and Variations

- Add another player or two. It'll give you other people to laugh at while you take a well-needed break between trips across the gauntlet.

- Use fewer columns, but make the player start over from scratch (replacing his correctly guessed card pairs with fresh ones from the deck) when he makes a mistake.
- Rather than using rows, simply guess whether each card flipped from the deck will be higher or lower than the last. Incorrect inklings incur a number of sips equal to however many cards are in the pile. Switch the guessing at regular intervals of cards or after so many right/wrong guesses. This version is sometimes called Hi-Lo.

Between the Sheets (a.k.a. Acey-Deucy): The dealer turns up two cards and the player bets a number of sips that the value of the next card flipped up will be between those two. If an ace is one of those first two, the player needs to call it high or low. If wrong, the player pays the price—double for matching up either of the first two cards. If right, he gets to give out that many drinks. If too wimpy to bet anything, he takes a gulp to pass. If successful in betting ten or more sips, the player can exchange his winnings for the right to create a rule.

Dice and Deck: You rocket scientists out there will note the addition of a pair of dice to the list of required equipment. The rules and set-up are very similar to Between the Sheets. The big exception is quite simply that you're betting whether you can roll a pair of dice and have the total be between the two cards flipped up. If doubles are thrown, the win/loss is doubled. For this one, aces are worth one, jacks eleven, queens twelve, and kings thirteen. If the two cards drawn are a pair, the player can either sip 'n' pass or add two cards and play both sets with different sip bets but only one roll of the dice.

B. S.

- Required: A deck and four to eight masters of the golden shovel.
- Summary: Get rid of cards each round based on whether (you're lying that)
  they're of a certain value.

Playing: Cattle feces, what does it really have to do with lying? Are bovines known for faking out ranchers with faux poo? Does it have something to do with rodeo clowns? Excretory etymology aside, it's not surprising that several games out there share the moniker. Lying and gaming go together almost as well as lying and drinking. Not to mention the fact that it's a real hoot to bellow "B.S.!" at people in an otherwise light-hearted social setting. It's just a fun word. And in this case, it denotes a card game with thirteen rounds, one for each card value ace through king.

The pack is dealt out. In each round, players toss in (face-down, at the same time) as many appropriate cards as they claim to have for that round (e.g. threes in round three or jacks in round eleven). When more than four of certain cards show up, that obviously means someone's trying to cheat, which really plays into the object of the game. If you suspect anyone is B.S.-ing (throwing down cards inappropriate to that round), challenge them. If you're right, they drink a predetermined amount or a penalty commensurate with whatever round it is. If you accuse falsely, you drink. Naturally, penalties should increase if questioning doubles or triples. After each round, be sure to sweep the cards, to minimize later confusion as to who threw what.

Strategy tip: Unless all your cards are eights or less, you'll need to lie if you want to win. With that in mind, it's especially helpful to try to get rid of your high cards in an early round. When playing inappropriate cards, you're less likely to get called to the carpet if you throw down amidst everyone. Typically, B.S.-ers toss in cards way before or after everyone else. Don't be scared about getting caught. It's part of good bluffing. You want folks to question you, especially if you have honest-to-goodness doubles or triples you plan to dish later. The more people who falsely accuse you early on, the less they'll doubt your veracity down the line. Which means if you mix up your actions—playing the right ones, wrong ones, and sometimes none at all, you'll do fine.

Whoever goes out first tells everyone else to drink. If those remaining wish to see the game through to the last round, let them. You'll find out which of your buddies is the most trusting, straight-laced non-aggressive person in the group. It's always good to know who they are. Those are the types you should pick as objects of the "How to Win Your Next Drink" tricks at the end of each section!

Seven and a Half (a.k.a. Sette Mezzo, Brain Damage)

- Required: A partial deck and two to six gambling goombas.
- Summary: Each player tries to get closer to seven and a half points than the dealer.

Playing: Remove all the eights, nines, and tens from the deck, then shuffle what's left and deal each player (including the dealer) one card face-down. From there, play resembles that of Blackjack. After each player bets (from one to a max of five drinks), he can add any number of cards that strengthen his hand without bringing the total over seven and a half. Court cards (jacks, queens, and kings) are worth half, aces are one and everything else (two through seven) counts as its face value—just different enough from the Golf game described earlier that the games will probably cause mass confusion if played back-to-back! In any case, any player who busts, by default has to drink his self-imposed penalty. Likewise, players lose to the dealer in the case of a tie. But on the bright side, the player automatically wins with a five-card Charlie (more than four cards without going over seven and a half). And finally, those who beat the dealer make him drink however much they bet—the maximum fiver therefore imposed as a precautionary measure, since in one round the dealer could potentially lose to several players consecutively!

Other Rules and Variations

- Try leaving in the black tens and making them wild—or perhaps, leaving in all the cards and making it that you just need to be closer to seven and a half, but don't have to be under. For instance, you could stay in with an eight (just half a point over) and actually wind up beating an otherwise strong dealer total of six and a half (a full point under).
- Either shift the deal clockwise around the circle after each round or make the dealer finish out the pack. (The latter, more harsh option is no doubt the origin of the less elegant non-Italian alias for the game listed above. If you choose that version, make sure you have a decent taxi service available in your neighborhood or a couch for that person to crash on.)

Screw Your Neighbor

- Required: Three or more shifty card players.
- Summary: The only card game imaginable where you try to avoid aces (being the high card).

Playing: From a shuffled deck, the dealer doles out a single face-down card to each player at the table. The player to the dealer's immediate left ponders whether or not to keep the card he received or switch with the neighbor to his left. Each player in turn gets a shot at swapping for a (hopefully) lower card with their neighbor. When the decision-making makes it all the way around to the dealer, he can either keep the card he winds up with or bury what he's got and take a fresh one from the top of the deck. The cards are revealed and whoever ends up with the highest for that round drinks a predetermined amount.

Strategy tip: The more people playing, the higher your card can be without you being screwed. In other words, if you're playing with three people, a jack is almost certain death; but with eight people, a jack may be the second or third highest card. So you'll always want to trade away anything ten or higher, but don't despair unless you wind up with that killer ace!

Because it's so quick and simple, it's a good warm-up game, change of pace, or end of the night game. And it works well with large groups. But if the group is more than five people, you might want to make it more interesting by having multiple losers each round.

If you like this one and haven't already checked out the Golf game described earlier, it's got a similar theme.

Under the Table (a.k.a. Oulies)

- **Required: Three coins for every person playing.**
- **Summary: Guess the total number of coins everyone's holding in their hands.**

Playing: With their respective coins at the ready, everyone dips their hands under the table and keeps between zero and three coins in their playing fist. The "dealer" then calls for all playing fists (only one per person) on the table. Players each guess aloud how many total coins will be revealed. Whoever guesses closest is out and doesn't have to drink with the others. Those who drink each owe gulps for either how many they guessed or the actual number of coins revealed.

Strategy tip: If you guess early, don't tip your hand by guessing low or high based on how many you've kept yourself. Do it based on whether you think people will be aggressive (figure two coins per person) or timid (figure one coin per person). If you're among the last to guess, just average the other guesses.

Other Rules and Variations

- Obviously, the number of coins each person can choose from can be adjusted inversely to how many people are playing (fewer for more and more for fewer).
- Whoever guesses closest can be out for the rest of the game. This might not be a great incentive to guess well, since that person just sits around; but it does help define how long the game goes on and you can make the last person left finish their drink.
- If there's a severe coin shortage, try using one coin per person, slapping the coin on the table and (with the coins still covered) guessing heads or tails. Not how many, just which there'll be more of. The majority wins and the minority drinks. If it's a tie, those showing tails drink.

How to Win Your Next Drink: The Three and Two-coin Line

The Set-up: Start with three coins of type A and two of type B arranged A-B-A-B-A. The size and type of coins don't matter, as long as you can distinguish them (e.g. by using heads and tails with five of the same coin). The challenge is, with only three moves, to get them into formation A-A-A-B-B or B-B-A-A-A. Since people assume sneakiness is involved, you need to be very clear about the fact that each legal move consists of:

- Moving any two coins that are both consecutive and touching.
- Not touching or sliding any other coins in the process.
- Leaving all five coins along the same line as they started.

The Trick: Move the second and third coins to the outside right (A-_-_-B-A-B-A); move the new third and fourth coins to the inside left (A-A-B-B-_-_-A); and then the new first and second coins to the inside right (B-B-A-A-A). A mirrored version of this solution (starting by moving the third and fourth coins to the outside left) will produce A-A-A-B-B.

The Ritual of Reacting to Exclamations and Gestures

Becoming a drinking game devotee is sort of like joining a private social club. One in which the dues required are that you know the proper responses to certain random stimuli. Learn well these pervasive possible set-ups and reactions, young Grasshopper, as they may be integrated into many games or just pop up spontaneously:

The Thumb: If you ever catch someone hanging a thumb on the edge of the table, react swiftly and quietly. Johnny-come-lastly has to drink. A common variation is placing a finger on the side of the nose (which can either be done at or away from a table). Better yet, try freaking out folks by making up a gesture, like a fist on your ear or both palms to your nipples. Half the people will look around, then rush to do it and half won't know what to do—either way, making them all look silly!

The Viking: The initiating player wiggles his Viking horns (thumbs in his ears), claps his hands together, and points at someone. As that player displays his Viking horns, the players on either side of him must animatedly row a mighty (invisible) Scandinavian vessel. A successfully coordinated three-person response allows the Viking to clap and designate another victim. Otherwise the entire trio has to drink.

Moose: Along the same lines as The Viking, except someone yells "Moose!" and points at someone. The moose, if on the ball, makes O.K. signs and holds his hands up to his face, making the moose's eyes. The players to his left and right must simultaneously respond with a respective antler (open hand, thumb in ear) to complete the moose's head. Any of the three who aren't quick enough or mess up their moose part must drink. Among other games, this is a popular occurrence in the ice tray version of Quarters (Cubes) described in Section 1.

Bull Moose: Not to be confused with The Moose, this is the completely different practice of drinking opposite-handed. For instance, if you're right-handed and you're caught drinking with your right, someone walks up and says "Bull Moose" and you have to finish your beer. (Because of the predominance of righties in the world, it might be safer just to make the rule Drink Lefty.) To keep things even more interesting, authentic practitioners reverse this rule between 12 and 1 a.m. If you're right-handed and you're not drinking with your right during that timeframe, someone walks up and says "Mull Boose" and you're caught. So stay on your toes!

The O.K. Sign: Basically, a running game of "made you look." If someone renders an OK sign below waist level (otherwise it doesn't count) and you're caught looking at it, you have to drink. The only way to block it is by (without gazing at it), penetrating the "O" with a finger. But beware, for those who practice this form of trick-drinkery are a cunning lot and it can be done just about anywhere with any set-up. (Best one I've seen was a guy pretending to play air guitar and looking down at his hand. He got five of us to look at once!)

Social: A bellow of "Social!" at any time is a call for everyone within earshot to repeat it, raise their glass and drink en masse.

Five-Second Drill: Pretty much the same as a Social, except with different words and a built-in time factor.

Incoming: A player cries "Incoming!" and gestures lobbing a hand grenade into the middle of where everyone's sitting. Whoever's the last to duck and cover drinks. If, instead, someone hurls themselves onto the invisible munitions on the bar/table—well, it's never happened before, so make up your own rule.

> **Side note:** To avoid killing the momentum of the festivities already in progress, you may want to limit some of these outbursts to only so many within a certain time period.

Using Animal Noises: The game Barnyard, described in the next section, is really the best example of how to spice up gameplay by imitating various woodland/farmside creatures. But those hoots, grunts, and oinks can also be integrated into any counting affair such as described in Section 5, in addition to such games as tag that follow.

SECTION 3: Crazy Talk and Silly Gesturing

A classic Hollywood example of this style of uninhibited mirth making can be found in the movie *Shanghai Noon*. A bonus feature on the DVD shows a translation of the words used in the animated game that its stars, Jackie Chan and Owen Wilson, play from within their tandem bubble-filled bathtubs. If two grown men in the Old West can let their guard down with such antics, surely you (and a few friends) can too.

Body Parts (a.k.a. This Is My)

• Summary: Ignore everything you know about anatomy.

Playing: Players take turns pointing to various parts of their body and naming any other part than that one they're pointing to. If anyone going around the circle screws up (by saying the correct body part or taking too long to make up a different one), they drink. Yup, it's just that easy. A nice, simple concept for the end of a long evening, versus some of the games that tend to take longer to explain than actually play. To make it harder, establish that players can't repeat any body part pointed to and/or named. (Not allowing one or the other, rather than both, actually makes it trickier.) If that's too difficult, you might have to practice by yourself at home in the bath.

Barnyard (a.k.a. Zoo)

- Required: Some playing cards and party animals.
- Summary: Moo, meow, hiss, bark, and bleet your way to triumph.

Playing: Deal out all the cards face down. Think back to the last time you were on the farm, at the zoo, or camping in the woods and some of the sounds that emanated from the surrounding creatures. Then share a good one with the group. That's the bestial noise you'll be known by for that round. Yes, wisenheimer, you can be whatever sound you think a giraffe is. Just as long as it's able to be imitated. Once you've gone around the table a couple of times and think you know everyone's animal utterance, begin turning over cards one at a time in a clockwise fashion. Any time two consecutive cards match (denomination and/or suit—whatever makes the game more fun), the two players immediately stand up and do the other's sound before they can do yours. If you hesitate or perform the wrong one, it's off to the beer trough for you. Maybe there you can take timeout to think about the heavy responsibility involved with being a more effective giraffe.

Sex, Drugs, and Rock 'n' Roll

- Summary: A sort of cross between the Alphabet Game and Rhyme or Reason.

Playing: In the regular Alphabet Game, players cumulatively name things that begin with each letter. For instance, consecutive players might say, "A is for Aardvark," "A is for Aardvark and B is for Bagel," "A is for Aardvark and B is for Bagel and C is for Chimes," etc. In Rhyme or Reason, it's not alphabetic or cumulative, but each response has to either rhyme or have an easily understood connection with the previous one. For instance, successive responses might be "Butcher," "Meat," "Greet," "Hello," "Yellow," etc. This game is similar to each of those in that it's alphabetical, but each response has to do with sex, drugs or rock 'n' roll. So folks might start with "Aerosmith," something beginning with "B" that relates to sex..., and "Cocaine"—which is a superb response, as it's both a drug and a Clapton song. The game can be cumulative or not, depending on your attention span. Needless to say, all of these games are about quickly blurting out topical words. So as you might guess, the penalty for drawing a blank, being slow or getting off the subject is taking a drag of your beer.

Frogs

• Summary: A mix of amphibians, arithmetic, and alcohol.

Playing: It isn't easy being green. And it isn't easy performing simple mathematical logarithms when you've been swilling beer...possibly from a green bottle? Okay, maybe that one's a stretch. But it's true. For example, just try to get through the following froggy phrase: "One frog, two eyes, four legs...in a pond...kerplunk!" Why would you want to? Again, when you're just sitting around drinking a brew and get bored, anything could seem like fun. In any case, any player engaging in Frogs who messes up this important zoological verse drinks. The game continues with players simply adding a frog each round. Naturally, that geometrically increases the numbers of eyes and legs. Likewise, the number of times you're supposed to say "in a pond" and "kerplunk" matches the number of frogs. For instance, the lucky landlubber who carries out the fifth round phraseology would begrudgingly croak: "Five frogs, ten eyes, twenty legs...in a pond, in a pond, in a pond, in a pond, in a pond....kerplunk, kerplunk, kerplunk, kerplunk, kerplunk!" In the end, more sad than the fact that a grown adult would utter this stuff is that several other adults would listen attentively to his every word in hopes that he'll make a mistake. Take my word for it. Don't make me say "I toad you so."

Whiz-Whiz-Boink (a.k.a. Whiz-Bang-Bounce, Rugby)

• **Summary:** The fast-paced pastime of passing a pretend hot potato.

Playing: Whoever's holding the imaginary ball tosses it up in the air and sets it in motion by proclaiming "Whiz!" and making a sweeping across-the-body motion to his left or right. Let's say, for example, he uses his right hand, sending the ball left. The player immediately to his left then needs to keep the ball in motion with one of these possible gestures:

- Another "Whiz" with the right hand (matching the direction the ball's coming from), which would keep it going left.
- A reversal "Bounce" with the left elbow (the direction the ball's heading to), which would send it back right.
- A mischievous two-elbows-in-the-air "Boink," which would preserve the ball's right-to-leftness but skip the next person.
- A dramatic "Bang," shooting anyone in the circle with the classic hand-as-a-gun formation, basically resetting the fantasy action.

Other Rules and Variations

- Other than a Whiz, only a Bang can start the faux sphere's trajectory. But since a Bang is basically a copout, whoever does the third one that round should really drink for being slow and unimaginative.
- Very important: Everyone has to properly announce the action they're doing as they do it.
- Whoever improperly identifies the gesture they're doing or isn't on the (invisible) ball, has to drink. Of course, if you're the guilty party who takes too long, just accuse the last person who "touched" the ball of knocking it off the table and out of your reach. They may just fall for your creative response...once.

Lasers: Same basic idea, but if you and your Battlestar Gallactica-loving buddies prefer to ditch the rock and whoop it up with make-believe laserbeams, go for it. Just point across your body (right-to-left or left-to-right) and send the beam on its way by making a "Bzzz" noise. Continue the beam on its magical journey with a similar point and "Bzzz" in the same direction. Or block it with a silent elbow move similar to the Bounce described above. For effect when performing one you can hold your wrists up like Wonder Woman deflecting a bullet, but two blocks in a row is illegal. If this "lite" version of Whiz-Whiz-Boink is still too complicated for you, maybe you shouldn't be allowed to play with imaginary gaming equipment.

How to Win Your Next Drink: Do As I Do

This simple-looking physical challenge is easy to do (if you know how) and guaranteed to leave your friends (who don't) looking silly and perplexed.

The Set-up: Tell them that all they have to do is copy you as you... Hold out your arms, turn your palms out, overlap your wrists, interlace your fingers, bring your hands in toward your body and up to your face, touch your index fingers to either side of your nose, unlace your other fingers and separate your hands, raise your elbows and reveal your pointers still glued to either side of your nose.

The Trick: Doing it correctly (winding up right finger to right side of nose and left to left) is all in the interlacing. As you interlace your fingers, instead of doing it naturally (so that the thumb of your upper hand is on the bottom), secretly shift the fingers of your lower hand one finger down and then interlace. Thus the thumb of your lower hand should be on bottom. After you swing the whole thing up and in, make sure your index fingers stay crossed as you unfurl them to touch the ol' schnozz. Feel free to repeat the process a couple of times to show off just how "easy" it is. Then just sit back and chuckle as your seemingly maladroit chums fumble around like fools.

SECTION 4: For Those With Skills

Each of these contests incorporates ordinary items found in most bars and at most parties. Plus, the game concepts are quite simple. So vanquishing foes in these tests of manual dexterity is sure to make them feel completely inadequate.

Spinner

- Required: A quarter, a table, and a flickin' finger.
- Summary: Keep the quarter spinning on the table as long as possible.

Playing: Catering for a moment to the majority of righties in the world, with your left index finger, hold the coin vertical and steady on the table; then give it a strong flick with your right index finger toward the very outside right of the coin. The more toward the center you hit it, the more you risk launching the thing completely off the table—as with all "sloppy dice," a punishable offense. In any case, that's supposed to be the easy part. The tricky part is that each player in turn has to then flick it to keep it going (or drink). The one allowable alternative—and this is where the Ooh's and Ah's come in—is that rather than continue the spin, a player if so inclined may, with a single finger (any finger they like), try to stop the quarter dead in the vertical start position mentioned above. Many such attempts will fail, but anyone talented enough to successfully do it gets to watch the last flicker drink, then starts the quarter a-spinnin' again.

Side note: Once you feel comfortable with your general coin spinning abilities, they can be used in conjunction with other games as a method for determining how long losers drink. For instance, someone playing Speed Quarters sends one off the table. When it's eventually recovered, shoot him a "Nice job, genius. Now you have to drink for as long as this quarter's spinning." With the flicking skills you've been practicing at home, you'll be able to give it a good twelve to fifteen-second ride. Much to the dismay of your poor, clumsy friend, who'll think twice the next time he bounces his two bits.

Matchbox

- **Required: Two to four players and one rectangular box.**
- **Summary: Drink (or not) based on how the tossed matchbox lands on the table.**

Playing: At first, it might seem more like random luck than skill. But when other players see the concentration in your foul-shot-like ritual each toss, they'll know you mean business. Most legal throws (attaining an apex of at least six inches above the table) will land the box on its broad, flat side. This is considered a failed attempt and the responsible player has to sip 'n' pass. If a player lands the box on its long, thin edge, it's worth two fingers (of drinking) to the next player who shanks one broadside. Likewise, to celebrate the rare occasion of the box coming to rest on its short, thin edge, the next player who falls flat owes four fingers. The only way to stave off drinking after a thin side is to consecutively land another one (long or short), which adds to the number of fingers in the penalty pot.

Strategy tip: Make sure there are matches in the box. They'll weigh it down a little and keep it from bouncing all over the place. Conversely, be sure to inspect the box if it's someone else's. The last thing you need is someone sneaking in one of those "loaded" boxes from Paraguay. That sort of chicanery may play fine down south, but really ruins it for the rest of us up here.

Throwing technique: The most successful one I've seen utilizes a single-finger launch. Palm up, hold the box with your thumb and middle finger on either broad side and your pointer on the short underside. Let go with thumb and middle finger, lift up with your pointer and spin the box up into the air. Done correctly, it could increase your thin-side frequency to about one in every seven tosses or better.

Other Rules and Variations

- If during the process any matches should fall out of the box, the offending player owes a sip for each match.
- If the box flies off the table (truly a display of weak technique), that's a two-finger penalty.
- If it lands in anyone's drink, that's a four-finger penalty.
- If you're in a pinch and can't locate a proper matchbox, trying to get a cork to land on one of its ends is a fair substitution. Or better yet, an unopened cigarette box could do the trick. But the only challenging part in this case will be to find a smoker who'll watch their cigarettes tossed around for more than fifteen seconds without grabbing one to light up.

Flying Cards

- Required: Aviation-ready cards and something to throw them into.
- Summary: Try to fling them into a distant hat, bowl, or shoebox.

Playing: At some point you've probably ventured to see how many cards from a whole deck you could get into a bowl from across the room. No doubt, the number of forty-six to fifty-one-card non-whole decks you've got left is a living testament to your (lack of) skills. But now that you'll be going up against another player in head-to-head competition, it's time to straighten up and fly right. With dueling decks and a bowl spaced equidistant, both players fire at will. If either player takes more than five shots without making one, he owes a drink for being generally untalented. When someone finally sinks one, he turns over his next card and the other player has that many attempts (jacks, queens, and kings warrant ten tries) to get one in. If he fails the challenge, he owes that many drinks. If he succeeds, the first player consumes. In the case of players sinking cards simultaneously and/or back-to-back, play is the same, except the drink burden doubles, triples, quadruples, etc. As you get better and cockier, you can drink more frequently for misses—every three or one, rather than every five.

Strategy tip: With your index and middle fingers along the long side of the card, hold it across the corner with your fingertips. From there, the two most popular throwing methods are underhand, which produces a fairly straight trajectory, and overhand, which is just as accurate, but produces a telltale S-curve flight pattern.

Caps (a.k.a. Stoppers)

- Required: Two bottles of beer, three caps, and deadly accuracy.
- Summary: Try to knock the cap off your opponent's beer.

Playing: Mind you, if you could do that to an unopened beer, you'd be extremely skilled—or more likely, using a bottle opener. But in this game you won't need to worry about that, because the beers are definitely already opened. The caps are placed upside down on top of the bottles and the players take turns throwing the spare cap. A player who topples his opponent's cap gets to go again until he misses, at which point the opponent drinks one finger for each time his cap was knocked off. Anyone decapping a foe three times in a row can make up a rule. (See Appendix B.) And if a player knocks off his own cap, he drinks a three-finger party foul. It's not so common when playing on a table. But when players use the classic diamond floor formation (legs in Vs, feet touching, beers in the crotch), it happens all the time.

Other Rules and Variations

- Adjusting your cap in between shots is a two-finger infraction.
- Getting your cap plunked by a player using the "snap" method carries a four-finger pricetag. In case you're not familiar, here's how to do it: Place the cap on the tip of your middle finger, put your thumb against the cap and finger, aim your elbow toward your target and snap hard. The force of the cap clanking the bottle may in and of itself be enough to knock off the cap! Then again, since misses with that method can both be painful and send caps flying in every direction, you may want to limit the use of that method.

Coasters

- **Required: Several cheap cardboard coasters.**
- **Summary: Flip 'em in the air and catch 'em.**

Playing: The basic set-up is hanging the coaster(s) over the edge of the bar or table. In round one, you'll flick one skyward with one hand and catch it with the other. Round two, try to flip and catch it with the same hand. For round three, set up two coasters side by side, at the same time whack one with each hand and try to catch each with that same hitting hand. In round four, hit two again, but catch them both with the opposite hand. Round five and on,

stack three or more coasters, smack them with one hand and catch as many as you can. Whoever fails or catches the least that round drinks the total number of coasters caught by everyone for that round. The only real strategy other than being quick and sober is to place your beer as far away from this action as possible. There's no reason why it should become an innocent casualty of this aerial war.

Mouth and Bottle

- Required: An empty bottle, willing piehole, and ample floor space.
- Summary: Pick up a bottle from the floor with that cavernous hole between your lips without falling over.

Playing: If it were just that simple, anyone with halfway decent flexibility could do it. But alas, this rivalry with gravity goes much deeper. Proper form dictates that the player hold one foot in the air and hold his ear with the other hand. It's highly recommended that this stunt be first attempted with a two-litre bottle, if you have one available. Hey, you gotta crawl before you can fall on your face, right? Of course, once you have no problem snatching the big plastic bottle with your oral crevice, you can make the limbo-like progression down to forty-ouncers, longnecks, twelve-ouncers, club soda bottles, and finally nips. Just don't set your sites too low too quick. Simply getting past the two-litre stage without losing teeth should be considered a win! Oh yeah, the drinking. Let's see... If the mouth in question comes up with the prize, everyone else drinks heavily. Otherwise, that player takes a pull. But chances are good you'll be laughing too hard at the player—wobbling around, mouth agape, ready to teeter over at any second—to really care about any further punishment.

The Cigar Game

- Required: Your favorite Cuban (or substitute thereof), a way to light it and those willing to take a puff.
- Summary: Whoever's holding it when the ash falls loses.

Playing: This one seems perfectly appropriate for wedding receptions. And any other classy celebration where people are way too happy to complain about the fact that they're choking on cigar smoke. So join in and look cool. Take a drag. And don't hesitate to finish your drink if you lose. That's what the others will expect. You can bet your ash on that.

63

How to Win Your Next Drink: The Dollar/Three-coin Snatch

Having once won twenty dollars from my friend Andy with it, I can honestly say that knowing this bar bet alone is worth the price of this book.

The Set-up: Place a beer bottle near the edge of the table. (You'll see why later.) Lay a dollar bill across the top of the bottle and stack three quarters neatly on top of that. Use as crisp a bill as possible. Make sure it's all centered on the bottle. And if the bill sags down on either side, take off the coins momentarily and lightly fold it lengthwise to ensure that it sticks out as straight and flat as can be.

    The challenge as you state it is: "Remove the dollar bill with one finger in one motion, without touching the bottle or disturbing the quarters." Remind them that it's not a goofy word trick and takes true physical prowess. After they fiddle around and knock the quarters over a few times, it's time to show 'em whatcha got.

The Trick: You'll want to be standing, for leverage. Lick the palm-side of your pointer finger, raise it about a foot above the coins and strike down-and-outward authoritatively, so that you hit the bill about 1½ inches (4cm) from the edge. If the motion is diagonal and swift enough, the moisture from your finger will provide suitable friction to grab the bill and leave the coins sitting pretty. If you don't put the bottle near the edge of the table, you might hesitate to hit the bill with the necessary force and follow-through, for fear of breaking your finger! Definitely practice this one until you can do it successfully at least two out of three times. Best of all, if you do mess it up every once in a while, it'll help the suckers to want to bet you!

The Ritual of Continuous Consumption

In the wide world of sports, you'll find athletes who can run faster and longer, jump higher and farther, hit harder and get drug-tested after races quicker. In the slightly narrower world of drinking games, we entitle these overachieving chug-a-lug champs "Anchormen." They tend to have a screw loose, but they're good people to know. In fact, they make the best allies when downing mass quantities is required in a team contest like Chandeliers or doubles Beer Pong. That's when they're at their best. Bringing up the rear, you can always count on an Anchorman to carry his weight.

But how quickly powerful allies can become archenemies! Such can be the case when all players present are called upon to do a "Waterfall." It's what's referred to elsewhere as a

"Board Meeting," a "Pinwheel," or "Chain Chug." All stand and the person who called it (usually having attained a special status) begins to drink. The person next to him cannot stop drinking until he does. It continues around like that until the last person, who's been drinking the whole time, finally puts down what little is left of his beer and gasps for air. Thus, as you can imagine, it's very bad to wind up on the business end of a Waterfall begun by an Anchorman!

Doing funnels, keg stands, and shotguns—power-drinking based on gravity and air pressure—may seem impressive. But these liquid binging flourishes will eventually hinder the Anchorman's ability to play any real drinking games. So by the end of the night, you'll have the last laugh. Unfortunately, by that time they'll probably be out back making a collect call to Europe on the big white porcelain telephone...

SECTION 5: Fun With Numbers and Counting

Even sober, most people are math-challenged. Without the aid of a calculator, they can't manage to balance their checkbooks—simple addition and subtraction. Perfect candidates to invite to play any of the following number-lovin' games.

Place Your Bets

- Required: A single die and up to six chance takers.
- Summary: Guess what number's going to come up.

Playing: Predictably, the person with the die calls out "Place your bets!" After a few statistical calculations, players announce their choices simultaneously by placing that many fingers on the end of the table. Not to exclude sixteen and two-thirds percent of the possible rolls, those endowed with five fingers per hand wishing to bet on six simply put a closed fist on the table. Every player who fails to guess the number has to drink that many sips. The die is passed after every roll. If a player happens to display Kreskin-like abilities three times in a row, he can make up a rule. (See Appendix B.) It doesn't matter if two people bet the same number. In fact, in theory you could allow folks to make two bets per roll, if they like. The caveat being that they'll obviously have to drink for both if they're both wrong. But if they get one right, you can make them drink half the penalty. The second hand thus acts as a sort of insurance, which must make prudent sense to you actuaries out there.

The Numbers Game

• Required: Three or more players with a keen knowledge of consecutive integers.
• Summary: Basic counting gone haywire.

Playing: The object is to sound off one to twenty. The counting starts clockwise. The first catch is that uttering two numbers in a row creates a reversal. The second is that saying three numbers in a row preserves the counting direction, but skips the next player. So it's especially confusing when, for instance, two doubles are followed by a triple. You need to pay close attention at all times! Anyone flubbing up the festivities quaffs one finger. And whoever gets stuck saying twenty gets to make up a new rule, but owes three fingers. To discourage dolts who want to make rules from ending on a double or a triple, make the penalty for doing so doubled or tripled.

Other Rules and Variations

- Replace certain numbers with letters, words, sounds, drinking, or even other numbers. You could wind up with a sequence that goes: "one," "Boo!," "three," "fourteen," "five, six," "seven," etc.
- Just as confusing, swap any two numbers. For instance, in swapping seven and eleven, the sequence could go: "five, six, eleven," "eight," "nine, ten," "seven," "twelve," etc.
- If it all gets too confusing, a general consensus (followed by a Social) can wipe the slate clean and start you over clean 'n' most likely not-so-sober.

Peter Plumbley Walker: As the legend goes, this version is named after a New Zealand cricket umpire who was killed in a bizarre bondage-gone-wrong accident that found his lifeless body resting in Huka Falls in the 1980s. So drink up, sports fans! The counting is done in Roman Numerals (I, II, III, IV, etc.). Well, sort of. In place of "I," players say "Peter;" instead of "V," "Plumbley;" and rather than "X," "Walker."

Thus nine (IX) would be "Peter Walker" and fourteen (XIV) would be "Walker Peter Plumbley." And if that's not morose and challenging enough, if the count should make it to fifty or one hundred, L and C are "Huka" (pronounced "Hooker") and "Falls," respectively.

Random: This is great on its own or as a follow-up to either of the above numberfests. It's a game of both initiative and fear. Rule number one is that there is no proper order in which players participate. As usual, someone goes first by saying "one." But then anyone can step in and say "two" and interject "three," etc. Rule number two—the kicker—is that if multiple people speak at the same time, they drink. Finally, rule three is that if more than two seconds of silence elapse, the last person to say a number shouts "Freeze" and selects someone to guzzle two gulps. If anyone lets out a peep while "Freeze" is being shouted, they owe three big gulps. Otherwise, the count is reset and the freezer starts it off again with "one."

Split the Difference (a.k.a. Lowball, Rolling Math)

• Required: Two dice and two math prodigies who can "minus stuff."

Playing: Each player rolls one die. The person with the lower number breaks out the abacus, subtracts his number from the higher number and takes that many drinks. When doubles inevitably come up, both players kick back the total of the dice. If it were any simpler, it wouldn't really be worth writing about. For that reason—and since a lot of drinking can take place in a short span of time—you'll probably want to play this as a quick "filler" between other games.

Fives

• Required: Five dice and three to five pent-up rollers.

Playing: One player throws all five dice. Any fives (singles and/or multidice combos) are put aside and that player rolls the remaining dice. If any fives come up as in the first roll, they're removed from the rest. It keeps going like this until a roll where no fives are made. Add up the dice that are left and that's that player's score for the round. After every player's had a turn, the one with the highest score in the round drinks. This can be a predetermined amount, their total for the round or the entire contents of a spare cup that was filled by the loser at the end of the last round.

> **Side note:** No matter how careful players try to be, this game will produce a glut of "sloppy dice." So be ready to grab them as they whirl around the table. Even with this warning, you're likely to spend half the time fishing around for them on the floor.

Hourglass

- **Required:** A deck of cards, a marker and four to six time travelers.
- **Summary:** Different cards indicate moving back and forth on a clock face.

Playing: Okay H.G. Wells, it's time to forge a card-based timepiece. That means arranging an ace through queen in the traditional one through twelve o'clock positions. It doesn't matter what suit they are, just set a dozen denominations in a pretty circle. Deal out the rest of the cards and make sure they're kept face-down. The marker (a chip, coin, key, priceless brooch, whatever) starts on the queen. Play begins with the player to the dealer's left turning over one of his cards. That sends the marker to that position (jack to eleven o'clock, three to three o'clock, etc.) counterclockwise if the card is black and clockwise if red. The player then takes drinks for the number of spaces the marker moved. If during its jolly journey, the marker crossed the Queen, the player gives the drinks instead. For instance, let's say the marker's at two o'clock and the nine of spades is turned. It goes backward, crosses His Majesty and that player gives away five drinks to the player of his choice. If the card pulled had been the nine of hearts, the marker would've gone forward and the player would've had to guzzle seven gulps. Play continues with the player to the left flipping up a card.

Other Rules and Variations

- When a queen is pulled, the marker shoots over to her and that player gives away double the normal dosage.
- As whenever giving out drinks, a player can split the punishment between multiple recipients.
- The player who turns up a king does nothing. But the next person to expose a non-king doubles the normal penalty. If more than two kings in a row are drawn, the fine triples or quadruples.

Crazy Eights (a.k.a. Eights)

- Required: Four to six players with cards and counting skills.
- Summary: Place (near) consecutive cards of each suit in the proper row.

Playing: Start the insanity by removing those four wacky eights and lining them up in a single column. Deal out the rest of the cards. (Players are permitted to look at their hands.) Each turn, players place a card into its proper row (by suit). If possible, the aim is to lay down something sequential to what's already there. A player who does this gives out the number of drinks for how many consecutive cards that makes. For instance, in the spades row, let's say you place the six into an existing sequence of the five, seven, eight, and ten. You'd get to hand out four sips for the five-through-eight run. If unable to put down anything in order, the player throws something close and must take as many sips as that number is far away from the closest card. In the example above, if the only spade you had left was the two, you'd play it and take three gulps. Since more drinks are handed out as the game progresses and the gaps are filled in, as with most games you can split the drinks given between multiple players. Which is important to keep in mind along the way, since those vengeful thirteen-drink sentences have a way of sneaking up on you!

Other Rules and Variations:

- Aces can be played high or low.
- Force folks to follow suit or lay down red and black every other one. Their inability to follow along will make for more taking of sips, rather than just the typical give-fest.

How to Win Your Next Drink: A Mathematical Prediction

The Set-up: Claim that you can read someone's mind.

The Trick: Tell your spot to think of the number representing the month in which they were born, add one and double it. Have them subtract their birth month number once. Then have them subtract it again. Now double the result they're left with. At this point, if they've done it right, they'll have the number four in mind.

Tell them to translate the number they're left with into a letter in the alphabet (e.g. A for one, B for two...Z for twenty-six). Ask them to think of the very first country that pops into their mind that starts with that letter (in this case, D). Tell them to use the second letter in that country name and think quickly of what animal starts with that letter. Have them focus on that animal's color. At this point, you announce that they are thinking of a gray elephant in Denmark. For the majority of times it works, folks will be so awestruck, they won't mind paying for your next round!

Side note: Unfortunately, it's in the nature of some people to go out of their way to foil you. They may have heard it before and want to try to purposefully (against your "whatever-you-think-of-first" orders) think of something different. Or just be a pain in the ass. So you may hear "a brown ostrich in the Dominican Republic" or "a white jackrabbit in Djibouti." But more often than not, the bigger risk is someone not following the math computations. In cases where you (think you might) run into this, try this sillier, simpler logarithm instead: "Think of a number...the number five. Concentrate on that number five. Now double it, add two and divide by three."

SECTION 6: Secret/Learn-As-You-Go

As the secrets within these games are revealed, you will either earn yourself the deep respect of your peers, or be completely humiliated. Try to avoid the latter as best you can, despite the fact that a confident, know-it-all attitude works best when initiating them—both the games and your friends, that is!

Rules of the Game

• **Summary:** The definition of an insider's game.

Playing: Approach anyone at the soirée and query: "Do you know the Rules of The Game?" The proper response is: "Why Sir [or Madam], it would be rude not to." If they come back with anything other than a reasonable facsimile of that, tell them to drink and walk away. If they come up with the right answer, flip a coin. They'll call it in the air. If they're wrong, they drink four fingers, otherwise you do. If they don't call it in the air, shake your head disappointedly, tell them to drink and just walk away.

Who Is It?

• **Summary: A game of mystery and misdirection.**

Playing: After announcing the name of the game, you tell everyone they'll need to concentrate and use their powers of deduction. Call attention to any three objects in the room. It doesn't really matter which, but you do want everyone to think it matters. So study the room, then slowly utter the "clues" as though you're carefully revealing key pieces of a complex puzzle. ("Okay, let's see. Mike's shirt...the fireplace...and...that Nintendo controller.") At that point, pause thoughtfully and question the group, "Who is it?" Whoever guesses wrong has to drink. Wait until several guesses have been made and there's an awkward silence, then try offering another set of three objects.

Strategy tip: It's especially deceiving when you include a particular person's clothing somewhere in the first set and restate one of the previously mentioned objects in the second set.

If no one guesses who it is after the second set of clues, tell them who it was and start another one. Oh, by the way, the correct answer is whoever speaks first after the words "Who is it?" So technically it could even be someone who isn't playing! Since it ruins whatever silly logic exists in the game, it's best not to restate the question until you move on to another round. Usually by the second or third mystery person, people catch on—or get bored—or beat the living daylights out of you. So try to feel out the crowd, throw a real clue in every once in a while, and make sure that whatever location you happen to be playing at has plenty of bandages on hand.

Side note: If someone else brings up the game, just play along. Even though you could quickly end the game by shouting "Me!" (the correct answer) right after the question, you'll look like a real jerk. So be a sport. Besides, it's almost as fun to yell out answers you know are incorrect (like other people in the bar) just to get people thinking!

Welcome to My World

• **Summary: Name items that fit the secret, unspoken pattern.**

Playing: As the ruler and host of your domain, you proclaim something to the effect of: "Welcome to My World. You must offer something worthy to earn entrance to this glorious kingdom. I already have a [name an object]. What do you bring?" Each player who—fingers crossed, hopes to join your lucky minion—guesses an appropriate addition. If they've played before, they know that what's apropos depends on the linguistic trend you've just set. They also know that it's most likely to play off one of the following:

- Two of the Same Letter: This one's pretty obvious to pick up on. As soon as you say you've got "Six Saxophones" or "Luscious Lettuce" or "Special Salsa" someone will get it. So if you're feeling generous, you can lead with this one.
- Your Initials: I (with initials ST) might insert "Secret Tomatoes" or "Silver Triangles" or "Skilled Tarantulas." You should be ready to defend particularly nonsensical responses.
- Just Your First Initial: If rather than on both initials, it's just based on your initial initial, that would beget one-word answers like "Sunglasses" or "Schnitzel" or "Starfish." Don't allow two-word answers.

• Last Letter Starts the Next Word: In this version you might hear the sequence "BanjoS" then "Suntan oiL" then "LicoricE" then "Elvis costello's doG" then "Gravy."

Whatever pattern's established, make sure players know that they only guess once per turn. If they guess wrong, they drink. If they guess right, neither you nor they say what the actual rule is! That ruins the game for everyone—especially folks who've never played and have no clue what's going on. You can help encourage folks to keep their yappers shut if they think they know it, by telling everyone that the most fun is watching players get it right one round by accident and completely lousing it up the next!

Other Rules and Variations

· A more casual, less vainglorious approach (than Welcome to My World) would be to say you're "Going on a Picnic" or a "Camping Trip" or a "Slow Boat to China" and ask folks what they'd take with them.
· To make sure someone's gotten it, you can ask them for another item they'd bring along. To be fair, give them a couple of seconds to respond, since you're putting them on the spot.
· Play until either everyone gets it or the interest level seems to be dwindling. At which point you can proclaim that you're feeling moody, everyone's banished, and must regain admittance. Then enact another of the patterns above or make up something on your own, your heinous.

Strategy tip: One way to keep the game moving is to employ a confidant—that is, a player who you place in the know. Before the game starts and away from the other players, let them in on the game's secrets. Plant them a few players away from you in the circle and signal them when to give a correct answer. Or better yet, since the timing is very important, tell them to start the game and you be the confederate!

Two Up/Two Down (a.k.a. Up 'n' Down, Up-Down)

· **Summary: Know the location of your limbs.**

Playing: Announce the name of the game and find out who already knows it. If it's only one or two out of a half dozen or so, that's fine. You proceed, "For those of you unfamiliar with it, it's real easy. You have three choices. When it's your turn, you either say "one up, one down;" "two up;" or "two down." Ask a player which they think it is. If you need to remind them of the three choices, especially early on, they need to drink. If they are correct, you congratulate them—even if they don't know why they're right—and tell them they're out for the rest of the round and must be silent. You proceed with each player around the table. Based on how your arms are positioned, that's the proper answer. The "up" referring to whether or not your arms are on or above the table, "down" meaning below. As you shift in your seat, the correct answer changes! As usual, needless to say, whoever answers wrong drinks.

Other Rules and Variations

· To be especially cruel and in-your-face, have it be based on each player's own positioning, rather than yours.
· If folks seem to be catching on too quick, reset and have it be based off the positioning of your legs or a third player (such as the one to the right or two to the left of the player in question, for instance).

Big Fat Hen (a.k.a. One Red Hen, Turtle Master)

· Required: A good memory and a cooperative tongue.
· Summary: Folks repeat a series of up to ten crazy phrases.

Playing: As the leader, you are charged with having memorized the entire following passage beforehand:

A big fat hen
And a couple o' ducks
Three brown bears
Four running hares
Five frisky felines frolicking
Six swans swimming sideways
Seven salty seamen swiftly sailing the seven seas
Eight elongated elephants elevating elegantly in an elevator
Nine naughty nuns kneeling nimbly in their nighties
Ten twins twirling twelve tricky twitching twigs triumphantly

Begin by beckoning, "A big fat hen," which each person in turn repeats. Each round after that is cumulative. In other words, each time around the room you reveal another freaky phrase and folks have to repeat all the phrases they've heard so far. Whoever can't remember or messes up along the way drinks. As their patient leader, you must repeat the correct version and allow them to do it until they get it right (or finish their beer).

It completely destroys the mystique of your social omniscience if you bring along this book and simply read from it. But there's definitely some leeway in terms of what you come up with in the moment of truth. Just be sure to involve numbers and tongue-twistingly awkward alliterations (often with animals). Most important, be consistent in what you say each time!

Other Rules and Variations

- Before "A big fat hen," some leaders encourage all to drink a group toast, "To the judge, Queen, and country."
- Rather than the T-filled phrase above, you may recite the random and potentially more raunchy tenth round verse: "I'm not a fig plucker, nor a pig plucker's son. But, I'll pluck fine figs till the fig plucking's done."
- "One Red Hen" is identical to "Big Fat Hen," save the first line. And I have no clue why the game is sometimes called "Turtle." It really has nothing to do with tortoises, as far as I can tell. But what do I know? I'm just a fig plucker's son.

How to Win Your Next Drink: Snaps/Guess The Celebrity

When performed well, this is the most bamboozling bar bet this book has to offer. But it's a two-man gig, so first you'll need to wrangle a worthy partner in crime. You must both have keen senses of intuition and improvisation—and know a bunch of famous people's names. My friends Mick and Jon have honed their abilities to the point of being uncanny. With a little practice, you too will befuddle folks far and wide.

The Set-up: The two of you ask a random victim if they'd like to play "Snaps." Your partner then walks away for a bit. The victim whispers any celebrity's name into your ear—let's say it's Tom Cruise. You signal your partner back and without uttering anything else, say something like: "The name of the game is Snaps. Try and guess. The name of the game is not

Snaps. Celebrities are what it's about. Ready? [snap, snap, snap, snap, snap] [pause] [snap, snap, snap] See what I'm saying? [snap, snap]." It seems like gibberish, but chances are pretty good that before you began the second set of snaps your partner would have shouted out the correct answer.

The Trick: After you say "The name of the game is Snaps," whatever letter starts the next sentence is the star's first initial. In this case, the "Try and guess" meant a T (for Tom). Likewise, after "The name of the game is not Snaps" whatever letter starts that sentence is the star's last initial. From there, you continue to spell out the rest of the last name (until your partner guesses it). Along the way, you indicate each consonant by starting a sentence with that letter. For vowels, you snap your fingers between one and five times. Never start a sentence with a vowel, even if it's one of the initials. Rather, snap once for "A," twice for "E," three times for "I," four times for "O," and five times for "U." Thus, this is how the clues above play out:

"Celebrities are what it's about."	C
"Ready?"	R
[snap, snap, snap, snap, snap]	U
[snap, snap, snap]	I
"See what I'm saying?"	S
[snap, snap]	E

There you have it, Mr. Risky Business himself. Hopefully it's easier to see why it was guessable with just the first initial and a few letters from the last name. (How many other "T. Cru's" can you think of?) In closing, here are some key pointers to keep in mind:

- The possibilities for consonant clues are practically endless, but the sentences themselves shouldn't be. The more concise, the less distracting for the person trying to remember all the clues given up until then.
- Vowels as initials are easier than vowels in the middle of names, since they can appear back-to-back, like the U-I in "Cruise"—or God forbid, in a vowel-heavy label like "Aiello!" This is why the MOST IMPORTANT THING TO REMEMBER is to deliver each sentence or set of

snaps in a quick burst followed by a pregnant pause. Otherwise, there's no distinction between the letters you're trying to hint at. Timing is everything here!

- The exception to only giving the first initial for the first name is if you're dealing with a one-word celebrity (i.e. "Madonna" or "Sting"). In that case, just say "The name of the game is Snaps" and spell out the name.
- For three-word names or folks known by a middle initial (i.e. "Tommy Lee Jones" or "William H. Macy"), you may want to do the following: "The name of the game is Snaps." [first initial clue] "The name of the game might be Snaps." [middle initial clue] "The name of the game is not Snaps." [last name clues]
- Just like you need to come up with a system of dealing with odd names, you and your partner need to work out a way of dealing with incorrect guesses. Hey, it happens! To minimize errors, have the receiver communicate some sort of O.K. (verbal or otherwise) after processing each clue, to indicate that he gets it so far. And when mistakes do happen, it's usually easier just to start over.
- Lastly, be sure to practice each role before actually attempting this in public. After a few sessions, you'll figure out that either you or your partner is better at giving or guessing. Go with your strongest set-up first and be prepared to switch!

The Ritual of The Penalty Beer

Sitting in the middle of the table, mocking you, ready to be consumed upon proof of your supreme incompetence is the penalty beer. It is the ultimate price to pay, with its offensive...

Size: The big multi-pint party cup; the pitcher; the fishbowl; the occasional cowboy boot.

Flavor: The swill beer; the flavored beer; the sickly sweet non-beer; the deadly mixture (beer, wine, whatever's lying around).

Stiffness: Tequila etc.

That's right, the penalty beer can be pretty harsh. Which is why before engaging in a game like Kings (where throughout the game players pour some of their drinks into the penalty cup), everyone should agree on a common brew to drink—or just use a neutral penalty beer. Such as with...

The Mushroom Cup: In any card game with discarding, rather than simply throwing them into a pile, place each discard atop the penalty cup so that at least two of the card's corners clear the edge. The ultimate effect of successively placing multiple cards in this fashion is a mushroom-esque branching out. The more cards, the better. In fact, half the deck shouldn't be a problem for even the semi-skilled. If someone knocks over a

few cards, they drink that many sips. If they knock over the whole pile, it's time for them to finish the penalty beer!

The Shiver Shot Method: Lick someone's neck, sprinkle a little salt on it, and give them a lime to hold betwixt their teeth. Then lick the salt, shoot the shot (from a glass or convex body area), and suck the lime. Now that's a punishment worth taking!

While all these crazy antics are going on, the rest of the people who didn't screw up royally need to busy themselves somehow. Which is why you'll often hear chants during the carrying out of the liquid sentence. Such as "Here's to Brother Jonny, Brother Jonny, Brother Jonny. Here's to Brother Jonny, who's with us tonight. He's happy, he's jolly, he's messed up, by golly. Here's to Brother Jonny, who's with us tonight." (Sung to the tune of "Here's to the Bus Driver" and substituted with "Sister" and/or the victim's actual name, in case you happen to know any of that.)

SECTION 7: Dumb Luck

No strategy or skill required. Minimal brainpower to understand and play. Just a matter of whether (mis)fortune smiles on you.

Across the Bridge (a.k.a. Drunk Driver, Forty Lordy)

- Required: A deck of cards and really good luck.
- Summary: Turn over as many cards in a row as you can without getting an ace or face card.

Playing: Give the deck a good shuffle or two, then deal out eight cards facedown in front of the victim—er, that is, player. Starting from left to right, the player flips over one at a time, trying to get across that "bridge" of cards. Any numbered card (two through ten) is harmless and the player continues flipping on his merry way. By contrast, an ace is the worst. The player who uncovers one must not only take four sips of beer, but also be given an additional four cards to traverse (dealt facedown, right-to-left, starting on top of the ace). Likewise, the number of sips owed and penalty cards for finding a jack, queen, or king along the way are one, two, and three, respectively.

Because of the tendency for play to weave back and forth with all the progressive flipping and penalty card set-backs, the game is sometimes called "Drunk Driver." And "Forty Lordy" because it's actually possible to owe a maximum forty sips for the unlucky sod whose penalties take him through the entire deck!

Side note: Given that sip sizes can vary, forty of them should collectively work out to at least two beers.

Other Rules and Variations

· Rather than eight, you can build a longer or shorter bridge. But don't be fooled. Although a ten-card row is very likely to yield thirty or more sips per crossing, a six-card bridge isn't much easier. You'd be surprised how many times a heartbreaking ace lurks under the very last card!
· Some folks who prefer a six- or ten-card bridge will form a three- or four-row pyramid. But that makes it more "Up the Pyramid" than "Across the Bridge."

Speedbump (a.k.a. Pay the Toll): The "Speedbump" added is a shot of hard liquor in the middle of the bridge. Play is the same as "Across the Bridge," with the added provision that any time you cross by the shot from left to right, the required toll is that you gotta knock it back. A word of warning: This can be a real killer and it's not recommended to play with more than a four-card bridge (two on each side of the shot)! Think about it. By definition, you'll have to at least do one shot as you pass by the first time. And chances are pretty good that you'll find a queen, king, or ace waiting for you on the other side, thus sending you right back. The worst hand I ever saw—and again, this is starting with just four cards—wound up with someone owing a leg-rubberizing total of four shots and eighteen sips of beer. As in real life, be careful not to let this "drunk driving" get you wrecked!

Peanut Races

- Required: Peanuts, beers, and a buoyant spirit.
- Summary: Drop nuts in your beers and watch them float up.

Playing: Let the shelling begin! In preparation for the festivities, remove the peanuts from their protective exoskeletons. Next, choose whether or not to peel away the brown skin and use a whole or half peanut—who knew this would be so complicated? Just make sure each person uses the same legumatory formation for the round. In fact, it might be a good idea to have an impartial party to referee. On their signal (something clever, like "three...two...one... DROP!"), everyone bombardiers their nuts into their beers. Whoever's peanut rises to the top last, drinks their beer. The rest just fish out their nuts and pop 'em in their mouths.

Other Rules and Variations

· Anyone who drops before the official signal drinks their beer.

· Anyone who, upon hearing the signal, misses their glass definitely drinks their beer.

· The winner of the round chooses the proper peanut form for the next round. Have the referee encourage players to make their selections quickly and efficiently.

· Anyone who theorizes out loud whether the brown skin and/or oval vs. flat-bottomed nature of the nut helps or hurts its buoyancy doesn't have to finish their beer, but should drink something and be told to shut up and get a life.

Trapped

· **Required: At least four non-claustrophobics and a deck of cards.**

· **Summary: Try to get rid of your cards by matching those cards played next to you.**

Playing: All the cards are dealt out. Whoever's hand includes the ace of spades plays it. If the player to his left can't put down another ace, he is then—dunh-dunh-DUNH—"trapped" between the players to his left and right. Starting with the player to the trappee's left, the players on either side of him take turns laying down one card at a time. The confined player owes a drink for each card he can't match. When Houdini finally does come up with an escape card, the player to his left must come up with a match himself, or be—dunh-dunh-DUNH—trapped! Once the first player goes out, every other player has to drink for however many cards he's left holding.

Strategy tip: Okay, so maybe there is a little strategy. If the person next to you is trapped, your best option is to match whatever card is played by the other trapper. For instance, if your co-trapper plays a three, you'd be wise to play a three as well, since the victim is guaranteed not to have one. If you can't do that, play one from a pair you have. That way, if it comes back to you, you're not trapped. Other than that, just guess!

Russian Roulette

- Required: Nerves of steel and either six cans of beer or six shot glasses and a little hard alcohol.
- Summary: The guts game.

Playing: Anyone who's seen the ultimately tragic downward spiral of Christopher Walken's character, "Nick," in the epic 1978 Vietnam saga *The Deer Hunter* knows the kind of mind-numbing suspense we're dealing with here. You've got a one in six chance. Do or die. Pull the

trigger and find out. So choke down that lump in your throat and give each of these a shot—er, that is, a try.

The Beer Hunter: A sixpack of any beer will do, but Coors Light seems especially appropriate. (You figure it out.) Ideally, you'll have six players. Disengage the cans from the yoke, ostracize one from the bunch, and pass it around. Each player does their impression of a paint mixer (being careful not to dent the can). The thoroughly shook-up can is mingled back within its brethren in a way that makes it as indistinguishable as possible from the other five. All six are distributed one in front of each player, who slowly grasps his can of destiny and raises it up under his nose. On the count of three, everyone cracks open their beer. The loser, needless to say, inhales and wears his. The rest can use theirs in whatever game is played next.

Indian Wrestling: This one's better for head-to-head competition. Obtain a sextet of small glasses—obviously, "shots" are most appropriate. Into five of them, pour plain old H$_2$O. Into the last one pour whatever your favorite clear spirit is (Peach Schnapps for example) or a mixture of them, if you wish. Player one carefully rearranges all the glasses while player two looks away. Player two then has the opportunity to do likewise with player one blind. And finally, with both players not looking, a third person (not playing) arranges the shots into a circle. Then the moment of truth. Both players reach for one and down it. If one of them was booze, one of the four remaining water glasses is dumped out and replaced with booze.

Either way, both players look away as the quartet is then rearranged. Both players turn around, grab and gulp. And then there were two... Again, if both shots left are just water, replace one with hooch. Now it's game time! The ultimate showdown. Somebody's got to bite the bullet this time—if they haven't already done so a couple of times!

Other Rules and Variations

- Both games can be played with more or less players. For more in Indian Wrestling, a fun twist is to make a side bet on who got the real shot.
- For best results in both games, setting the drinks on a lazy Susan and giving it a gentle whirl (mimicking a gun's chamber action) right before the selection would be a great effect. And some tension-filled classical music might help the ambience too.

Horse Race

- Required: A pack of cards and at least two to pony up bets.
- Summary: Your "horse" wins, places, or shows based on the suits of the cards drawn.

Playing: Remove the kings and queens and line them up in a single column of eight cards in no particular order. Line up the four aces perpendicularly just below and to one side of the bottom king or queen (so the cards form an "L," with the corner missing). Shuffle the rest of the cards. Now folks bet on which ace (each suit is a different "horse") they think will finish first. The race starts with the top card from the rest of the deck flipped up. The ace matching the suit of that card gets to move ahead one space (parallel to the kings and queens). The race continues by flipping up the next cards from the deck and moving along the associated aces. Whoever bet on the winning ace (to cross past the last king or queen first) gets to give out twenty sips. Those whose horses place or show (come in second or third, for you greenhorns) get to give out fifteen and ten sips, respectively.

Other Rules and Variations

• If you have more than a few folks betting, you might want to write down which ace each player's betting on, to discourage cheating.
• Even though there can be multiple winners on each horse, each one gets to give out the full amount of sips. In other words, the winnings are not divided.

How to Win Your Next Drink: A Matter of Simple Anatomy

This isn't one of those bar bets that relies on expert skills, esoteric knowledge, or fancy wordplay. Just the opposite, actually. It's deceivingly straightforward.

The Set-up: Challenge someone that they can't name all ten three-letter body parts in less than three minutes.

The Trick: No trick, but abbreviations ("D.N.A.") and slang ("gut," "pit," "bum," "ass," etc.) are not allowed. For some reason, most crass cretins come up with those first. In any case, the actual three-letter parts of the human body are: eye, ear, arm, leg, toe, lip, jaw, hip, rib, and lid.

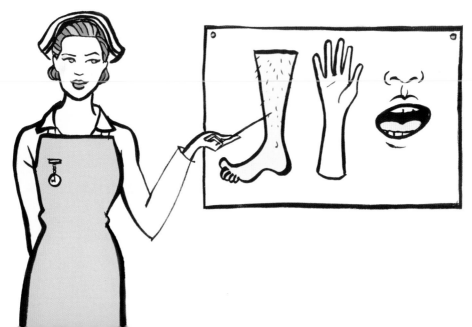

It's funny to watch folks scramble frantically, looking and pawing themselves over, trying to uncover the "hidden" answers on their bodies! Typically, the first five come easy. "Hip" and "rib" give people trouble because they're "inside" and not top-of-mind. "Jaw" and "lip" are a little tricky because you can't see them on yourself—unless you're Jay Leno or Mick Jagger. Occasionally some pre-med wannabe will challenge "lid" (as in "eyelid") and offer "gum" (in the awkward-but-semi-plausible-sounding singular) as the "real" tenth part. To be honest, neither of them are common physiological references. Probably the best way to settle this debate is to punch the smartass in the mouth and eye and see how they complete the sentence, "Ow, my ___ is swollen!"

SECTION 8: Check Your Reflexes

These are best played by folks who are ALERT and RESPONSIVE. In other words, if it's toward the end of the evening, don't even bother!

Taxi Driver

- Required: A driver (dealer), some passengers (players), and a set of wheels (cards).
- Summary: When your number comes up, you're either in or out of the cab.

Playing: Starting with the player to the dealer's left and beginning with "two," players each call out consecutive numbers, which will serve as their "stops." The dealer then flips over one card at a time. If the number corresponds to a passenger's stop, that player is "in the taxi" until his card comes up again. In the meantime, other players may join him in the taxi. As long as passengers are in the taxi, any time a face card shows up, they must drink. Just like in Across the Bridge (from Section 7), the values are four for aces, three for kings, two for queens, and one for jacks. Which is why it's important to pay attention and keep an eye out for your stop! If no one's in the taxi when a face card shows, the driver has to drink—which makes things pretty messy for those along for the ride.

Taps

- Required: A coin for each player and a table you don't mind marring.
- Summary: Players take turns tapping their coins on the table.

Playing: Whoever called the game starts by tapping once to send play to the right. The person to the right then can either tap once to maintain that direction or twice to send it back the other way. A player must drink if he taps out of turn or fails to tap soon enough (based on a consensus, but usually two seconds is more than enough time to allow). As you can well imagine, this game's really quick and easy and probably shouldn't be played for more than a few minutes.

Other Rules and Variations

- To make it interesting, you could define other tapping patterns, like that triple-taps skip the next person or that "tap-ta-ta-tap-tap" sends it across the table, etc.
- You could say that a certain sequence of taps (a single, followed by a double, followed by a triple) means whoever's the last to quickly tap five times right after the sequence has to finish their beer. That way you keep people on their toes!

Catch The Pig (a.k.a. Chase the Ace)

- Required: A pair of dice and at least four swine seeking to scramble.
- Summary: Try to roll a one and not get caught with both dice.

Playing: The dice are given to players sitting across the table from each other. Play begins with the other players loudly chanting "Catch...the...Pig!" At which point each die is rolled as many times as it takes to get a one. When a one is scored, that die is passed clockwise to the next player. If a player gets caught with both dice in front of him, he's "the pig" and must pay the penalty. Play continues with the pig keeping one die and the other going to the player sitting opposite him.

Strategy tip: If you like to live life on the edge, try hogging one of the die. Especially when you're playing with more than four people, it's fun to hold onto the die, look at it, contemplate its cubic nature, and then roll slowly when the other dice approaches within a player or two of you. After you hit a one, pass that die, get the other die, and roll that one quicker. The idea being that it gives you a better chance of your neighbor becoming el puerco— versus you.

Other Rules and Variations

- If a die should leave the playing surface, no one is obligated to help the sloppy player pick it up. Although it's fun to keep it from him, it's still pretty mean!
- You can either have a set penalty or have the caught pig roll both dice and drink the total. Even more hardcore, have them owe shots for how many times it takes them to get a one with both dice!

Circle of Death (a.k.a. Connection, Ring of Death)

- **Required:** Three or more players with a death wish and a deck of cards.
- **Summary:** Matching consecutive cards' suits or numbers is a bad thing.

Playing: The dealer spreads the deck facedown in the form of a circle. The player to the dealer's left turns up a card. The player to his left turns up another. If the two cards are of the same suit or value, each player has to drink. The next person clockwise then turns up a card. If it keeps the connection going, players drink for every connected card in front of them. For example, Player A flips the three of clubs, player B flips the seven of clubs, they both drink; player C flips the seven of hearts, all three drink; player A flips the jack of hearts, all three drink again and player A drinks twice; player B flips the queen of spades, no one drinks; player C flips the two of spades, B and C drink; and so on.

Other Rules and Variations

- The penalty for matching could be based on the card's value (aces being one, jacks eleven, queens twelve, and kings thirteen) or suit (spades worth one, hearts two, diamonds three, and clubs four).
- The player who breaks a connection has to also take a gulp.
- Tree-o-Rama is basically just Circle of Death, but using the "Mushroom Cup Method" of discarding discussed in The Ritual of the Penalty Beer.

How to Win Your Next Drink: The Quarter/Bill Balancing Act

The Set-up: Bet someone you can balance a quarter on the edge of a dollar bill for a solid three seconds. As with most tricks like this, it'll be most effective to borrow the bill and coin from someone else, in order to show that you're not using "magic" props.

The Trick: Put a little crimp just above the president's head. You don't need to fold the bill all the way in half, but just enough so that it rests on the table in a V. Then balance the center of the quarter over the corner of the V. Now the tricky part. As you carefully pull apart the ends of the bill to straighten it out, lift it ever-so-gently off the table. The quarter will stay centered on the crimp, so long as you don't pull the bill completely taut. You may surprise yourself the first time you do it, but don't be so shocked that you forget to give the standing three-count out loud!

The Ritual of Combining Games

Even with an exciting selection of drinking games to choose from, some people are just never satisfied. Yes, it's possible. Certain unnamed malcontents merge different contests into such popular games as Kings (from back in Section 1).

For the sake of variation, folks make room for certain mini-games by changing around the defined values for which numbers indicate giving and taking drinks. Thus, these tricky mixers play that certain numbers indicate the beginning of a Waterfall or session of Speed Quarters or such other quickies as Questions (respond in turn to each interrogative with one of your own), I Never (admit something weird you've done based on disagreeing with another's leading statement), Story (word by word, one player at a time, improvise a tale that makes sense), or others. The common thread being that whoever breaks the chain during the diversion has to drink; and then the game goes back to normal.

Sometimes the combination is an augmentation, as when using the Mushroom Cup method of discarding described in The Ritual of the Penalty Beer, just before Section 7. Another example being the game Liquid Hell, which combines the fun of Up and Down the River (from Section 1) with the potential pain of Across the Bridge (from Section 7). The dynamic is that the Across the Bridge game is used as a post-River penalty—in this case, for the person with the most cards left in their hand. Yes, it's cruel. And yes, as the rules go, if there's a tie in having the most cards left, both players do it.

Finally, other games are a direct melding of two or more other popular games. For instance, another version of Drunk Driver is a cross between Gauntlet (from Section 2) and Across the Bridge (from Section 7). Six cards are dealt facedown in a line. The player chooses which end he wants to start from, the card at that end is turned up and he has to get safely across by correctly guessing whether the next card in line will be higher or lower. Each incorrect guess means the player drinks two to six drinks based on the position in line of which one he guessed wrong, plus he has to start over. Like with Gauntlet, the penalty doubles if the same card shows up. And other cards can be assigned as big fines or automatic stoppers. The victim wins if they make it across with five successful guesses (ending on the sixth card). If they don't do that by the time the deck's done, they're officially declared a drunk driver and have to finish whatever drops of beer they have left. As with many typical combo games, this one can get pretty nasty pretty quick. But that's a small price to pay for such a thrilling amalgam of drinking games.

SECTION 9: The (Drin)King of All Media

Playing media-based drinking games while you listen to music, watch television, or see a film is a great way to double your entertainment pleasure! One well-known application is called The Magic Word. You simply pick a much-repeated word or catchphrase from a song, movie, or show and drink every time that word or phrase is uttered. The classic example was drinking every time someone said "Hi, Bob" during the old Bob Newhart show. But you can probably think of tons of other examples from Bob Dylan ditties to *Friends* episodes to *Police Academy* movies, along with various other favorites. *

*See Appendix A for clues on how to make up your own TV/Movie games.

Music: Being the perceptive creature you are, you probably noticed that bar owners and party hosts tend to crank up the tunes. Which is probably a big factor in why music-based drinking games are so popular. For instance, the informal Name That Artist dictates that if you're the first to shout out the band responsible for the song that just came on, you can tell others to drink. But you can't wait more than ten seconds into it; and if someone comes back with the correct song title before you, the penalty's reversed. Once you've got that down, the big leagues version is hitting the scan button on your radio and trying to name every song you can before it jumps to the next station. On the tail end, the final classic music-based drinking game, Until the Song's Over, uses the length of a song as a measure of time. That is, you have to finish your beverage before the current song ends—which, if the genre happens to be rock 'n' roll, probably means you've got less than three and a half minutes to go.

TV and Film: Similar to the Magic Word, Your Character means that you consume whenever your character shows up on screen, gestures in a certain way, or speaks any of a number of catchphrases. The best part here is that your character doesn't even have to be an actual person! It could be seeing a shot of the ship on *The Love Boat* or hearing the "DUNH-DUNH" sound on *Law and Order*, or witnessing the act of Captain Kirk getting on his groove thing with that week's lucky female alien in classic *Star Trek*. By contrast, Actor and Movie is more trivia-based. One person names an actor or actress and each person in turn has thirty seconds to come up with another movie that actor or actress appeared in. Anyone who fails to name an appropriate credit has to drink for each one already named, plus each subsequent film the other players can generate in the next thirty seconds. Lastly, anyone who's heard of The (Six Degrees of) Kevin Bacon Game, knows Star Connections. The only differences being that it can include both TV and movie credits (if you so choose) and Kevin Bacon doesn't have to be involved. In other words, you might challenge someone with something like, "I can link Bugs Bunny to Pee Wee Herman in five movies." If they can't beat that (by linking with fewer movies), you win and they drink—that is, once you spout off something like, "Bugs Bunny to Christopher Lloyd in *Who Framed Roger Rabbit* (one), Christopher Lloyd to Jack Nicholson in *Chinatown* (two), Jack Nicholson to Tom Cruise in *A Few Good Men* (three), Tom Cruise to Valeria Golino in *Rain Man* (four), and Valeria Golino to Pee Wee Herman in *Big Top Pee-Wee* (five)."

How to Win Your Next Drink: Best Bar Trick from the Movies

Like the games in Section 6, this is one of those bar tricks that will quickly earn you either the reputation of a clever, worldly fellow or a punch in the gut. It was performed in the 1996 film *Trees Lounge* by Steve Buscemi (who also wrote and directed the flick).

The Set-up: Buscemi's character, Tommy, challenges a fellow down-and-out barfly to finish a single shot of beer before Tommy can polish off two full pints. You probably have the same perplexed look as Tommy's challengee did in the movie. Which is why Tommy adds the following two simple (paraphrased) rules the challengee must go along with: "First, to make this sporting, I can't touch your glass and you can't touch mine. Second, since you obviously have a big advantage, you have to at least wait for me to completely drain my first pint before you pick up your measly little shot of beer to drink it. Fair enough?" Most people will agree to these conditions.

The Trick: The beers are poured and set on the bar. Everyone watches with anticipation as Tommy chugs the first beer. As soon as he finishes the last drop, he quickly inverts his mug and places it over the shotglass of beer sitting on the bar. According to rule number one, the poor sap can't touch Tommy's glass! Tommy now has plenty of time to finish his second beer, thus winning the bet. The big assumptions being that your challengee is a fair, level-headed sort and that you can get your glass over his, which means he can't be touching it while you're chugging your first one.

SECTION 10: Anything-for-Alcohol

Interestingly or sadly enough, with enough booze and a little creativity, pretty much anything can be made into a drinking game. Ordinary board games, video games, and other card games are easy enough to transform. Whenever you tank a round of Pictionary, get knocked out in VirtuaFighter, or give up a trick in Hearts, drink. As you consider the possibilities, contemplate the much more thoroughly entertaining drinking game that can arise during graduation ceremonies.

This assumes, of course, that you're either of proper drinking age by the time your big day arrives, or that it's not your graduation and you're just in the audience having fun killing time. Either way, take a sip whenever a speaker uses any of the following phrases: "Bright future," "deserving," "faculty," "fond memories," "hard work," "job," "knowledge," "late nights" or "all-nighters," "learning," "party," "perseverance," "sacrifice," "study" or "studies," "tuition," "vision," "volunteer," and of course, "drinking." Take a big gulp when someone quotes either a former president of the university, any political figure, or a current rock hit. And take a healthy swig if a speaker mentions any of the following: The great debt owed your parents; the length of time it takes to graduate nowadays; how hard it is to find a job right now; how many National Merit Scholars there are in this graduating class; any of the different surveys that rank colleges and universities; or how (un)affordable college in general, and your institution in particular, is. Finally, if a speaker makes a meaningless comment solely intended to draw laughs or a particular graduate's friends and relatives are tacky enough to yell and cheer when their name is read, drink until the laughter or cheering stops. Basically, when in doubt, drink. Hey, it's a joyous occasion!

To create your own game/joyous occasion, simply look for any situation where there's repetition, penalties, and/or competition. Within reason, stuff that doesn't require excessive

skill, reflexes, or on-the-spot intelligence works well. For instance, Boozed-Up Battleship or Slurred Scattergories, not a bad idea; Drunken Darts or Hungover Hang Gliding, definitely not a good idea. Team sports and crazy relay races are fun for about five or ten minutes when you're sauced and then things fall apart. But it's better than some of these drinking games that require completely impractical accessories, such as shopping bags, badminton equipment, seventy-two shot glasses, hot dogs threaded with twine, and other bizarre sets of items that don't tend to be lying around most bars and parties. Other than that, chances are pretty good that you could give up your day job and do nothing but come up with drinking games—literally, "ad nauseam!"

Appendix A: Popular TV/Movie Drinking Games

As stated back in Section 9, just about any movie or TV show can be made into a drinking game. All it takes is knowing the key characters and what they typically do and say. For instance, ever wonder if you're more likely to hear "Houston" in *Apollo 13* or the F-word in *Scarface*? Or if you'd have a better chance on a per-episode basis of catching Kramer sliding into Seinfeld's apartment versus Lenny and Squiggy barging in on *Laverne and Shirley*? Tough call, but it'd be fun finding out! In the meantime, here's a brief, admittedly inadequate, look at some of the more beloved clichés from the world of entertainment:

Stuff Worth Taking a Sip For

- Your character on screen. (Beforehand, each person chooses which character(s) they will "play").
- A common exclamation ("D'oh!" on *The Simpsons*, "Sharon!" on *The Osbournes* or "Yeah, baby!" from *Austin Powers*).
- A catchphrase ("Excellent" from *Bill and Ted's Excellent Adventure*, "Is that your final answer?" from *Who Wants to Be a Millionaire*, "...And this one time, at band camp..." from *American Pie*).
- A recurring theme (Clark Kent turns into Superman, Fletch uses another alias, Wile E. Coyote gets seriously injured, Bill Murray's character relives another day in *Groundhog Day*).
- A repetitive occurrence (Ferris Bueller turns and speaks to camera, someone loses a limb in *Braveheart*, Frodo puts on the ring in *Lord of the Rings*).
- Any character audibly burps or farts (a la *Revenge of the Nerds* or *Dumb and Dumber*).
- Robert DeNiro uses a word that starts with "F" and rhymes with "duck" (naturally, referring to his bandying of "firetruck" in the 1991 hit movie *Backdraft*).
- Anyone in the movie enjoys an alcoholic beverage. (A word of caution, be especially careful about trying this with *The Doors, Leaving Las Vegas, Arthur,* or *Fear and Loathing in Las Vegas*!)

Stuff Worth at Least Half a Beer

- A special character makes an appearance ("Q" on *Star Trek: The Next Generation*, "Colonel Flagg" on *MASH*, or "The Great Gazoo" on *The Flintstones*). This counts double for characters from other shows (Frasier showing up on *Wings* or Ren and Stimpy on *The Simpsons*) or ones who are often referred to, but never/rarely actually seen (Norm's wife Vera on *Cheers* and Jenny Piccolo on *Happy Days*).
- A vehicle does something cool (They jump to light speed in *Star Wars*, the General Lee jumps something in *The Dukes of Hazzard*, James Bond activates some fancy defensive weaponry in whatever car or boat he's being chased in).
- Any time there's a montage with no dialogue (like in a chase, when a couple is becoming romantically involved, or a detective is out deducing a series of clues).
- A glaring continuity flaw (between cutting back and forth, you notice a character's clothing, food, general position, etc. magically changes for no good reason).
- The characters in a horror flick decide it's wiser to split up.
- Any sort of nudity—hey, why not celebrate the human form and all its beauty, in a respectful situation?
- Any time the full title of the movie is uttered during the movie ("According to The Rules of Engagement..." or "We'll call these guys The Dirty Dozen" or "Gosh, that'd be The Perfect Storm"). This rule doesn't apply to movies like *Fletch* and *Shane* and *Forrest Gump*, where the title character's name is mentioned more than 739 times throughout the picture.

You get the idea. Pick and choose any from above and value them on whatever scale you want or feel free to add your own trigger events. By all means, certain less common stuff should call for a Social and/or consuming a greater quantity. Again, when making up your own from scratch, the most important thing is that you know the material and delegate drinking duties to each player as equally as possible. Unless that person is both clueless and deserves to be severely punished.

Appendix B: Typical Rules Made in Gameplay

Other than getting to watch your friends become gradually goofier as the night wears on, the ability to make up rules during play is one of drinking games' big rewards. It's a feeling of greatness to be able to spontaneously change the course of affairs. And since you don't want to blow it when you get your big chance, study the below list of popular rules established in typical gameplay. That way, you'll have a pretty decent idea of how to best abuse your fleeting power:

- No pointing.
- No swearing.
- No showing your teeth.
- The word "drink"—in any of its noun or verb tenses—cannot be used ("beverage," "consume," and "imbibe" are standard alternatives).
- Certain numbers aren't allowed. (See Fizz-Buzz in Section 1.)
- The words "glass" and "pint" are verboten.
- Players aren't to be called by their real names. Additionally, they can be called nicknames, other players' names, or anything you want.
- Everyone must speak with a particularly kooky accent.
- Players may only drin...that is, IMBIBE using a certain hand.
- Players need to get your permission, salute you (either with a funny phrase or made-up gesture), or remove a tiny imaginary creature from their beer each and every time before consuming.
- After speaking or being spoken to, players must utter a rote phrase, such as "Oh Master, My Master" or "Sir, Yes Sir."
- Cups must remain no further than a finger length from edge of table.

- Certain players must share the penalty every time certain other players violate a rule.
- Players can't leave to go to the bathroom without your permission (or a majority vote by the other players). Additionally, players may have to finish their beverages before heading to the can.
- Finally, if it's agreed that there are too many rules clogging up the flow of the game, the slate can be wiped clean by a quick vote.

As you can see, many of these rules are based on actions most players would do automatically without even thinking. That's the whole idea, Einstein! It tends to cause more violations that way—assuming somebody's straight enough to catch them. And in the end, you'll feel superior for playing a key role in that highly important and technical process.

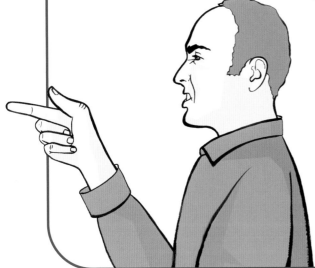

Appendix C: Toasts from Around the World

The most cultured complement to knowing a worldly variety of drinking games is having a global repertoire of phrases to say as you raise your glass. For example, if you're ever in such far away places as Indonesia, India, the Marshall Islands, Botswana, Uganda, or parts of South Africa, you'll find that "Cheers" is the common local toast. Whereas Europeans can often be found drinking to their health, with utterances such as "Prost," "Salud," and "Vashe zdorovie." By contrast, Asian versions (such as Japanese, Chinese, and Korean) tend to go for the direct approach with shouts meaning "dry your cup." And even closer to the source, in Scandinavia, the much-heard "Skål" literally translates to "drinking vessel."

Due to the wide assortment of tongues displayed overleaf, as many semi-phonetic pronunciation hints as possible have been included. ★ However, in lieu of doing true justice to any of the languages, just remember to raise your glass toward your drinking buddies confidently and make direct eye contact with everyone you can before the nectar hits your lips. (Naturally, this is more for special toasts than each and every sip required during the gameplay!)

Language	Toast	Pronunciation Hint
Afrikaans	Gesondheid	
Albanian	Shëndeti tuaj	"Shun-DAY-tea TWO-eye"
Amareegna (Ethiopia)	Desta / Letenachen	
American	Bottoms Up, Here's Mud in Your Eye, Down the Hatch	
Arabic	Fi sahitak	"Visa-HEY-duck"
Armenian	Genatset	
Asturian (Northern Spain)	Gayola	"Guy-OH-la"
Austrian	Prost / Zum Wohl	
Azerbaijani	Afiyæt oslun	
Basque	Topa	
Belgian	Op uw gezondheid	
Bengali (Bangladesh)	Joy	
Bosnian	Zivjeli	"ZHI-valley"
Breton	Yec'hed mat	"YECH-in-MOTT"
Bulgarian	Nazdrave	"Gnaw-STRAW-vay"
Cantonese	Ging jau / Yahm pai	
Catalan	Salut	"Saw-LOOT"
Chipewyan (Northern Canada Aboriginal)	Neybah sooghah wahley	
Chinese	Kong chien	
Cornish (The UK)	Yeghes da / Sowena	
Creole	Salud	"Saw-LOOT"

Croatian	Zivjeli / U zdravlje	"Zheeva-LEE" / "Ooze-DRAW-vlee-ay"
Czech	Na zdraví	"Nose-DRAW-vee"
Dagaare (Ghana)	YE nyOge ngmama	
Danish	Skål	"Sh-coal"
Dutch	Proost	"Pro-sht"
Egyptian	Fee sihetak	
Esperanto	Sanon	"SAW-none"
Estonian	Teie terviseks	"TAY-uh tear-vee-SEX"
Eurish (Neo-Latin)	Proea	
Farsi (Iran)	Ba'sal'a'ma'ti	"Biss-allow-ma-TEA"
Finnish	Kippis	"KEEP-pis"
French	(À votre) santé	
Frisian (in Netherlands)	Tsjoch	
Galician (North Portugal/Spain)	Chinchín / Saúde	"Tchin-tchin" / "Saw-OO-day"
Georgian (South of Russia)	Gaumarjos	
German	Prost	
Greek	Gia'sou	"YA-sue"
Greenlandic	Kasugta	
Hawaiian	Hipahipa	
Hebrew	Le'chaim	
Hungarian	Egészségedre	"Egg-GAY-shay-ga-DREH"
Icelandic	Santanka nu / Skål	"Sh-coal"

Ido	Ye vua saneso	"Yay-VOO-uh saw-NAY-so"
(Planned international language)		
Indian	Apki Lambi Umar Ke Liye	
Interlingua (A combination)	A vostre salute	"Ah-VO-stray saw-LOO-tay"
Irish Gaelic	Sláinte	"SLAWN-tchuh"
Italian	Alla Salute / Cin cin	"All-a-saw-LOO-tuh" / "Tcheen-Tcheen"
Japanese	Kanpai/Banzai	"Calm-PIE" / "BUNS-eye"
Korean	Konbe	"Come-Bay"
Latin	Sanitas bona / Bene tibi	
Latvian	Prieka	
Lithuanian	I sveikata	"Ees-fay-COT-uh"
Malaysian	Minum	"ME-noom"
Mandarin	Gan bei	"Gun-bay"
Mazahua (Ancient Western Mexican)	Shípi	
Mexican	Salud	"Saw-LOOT"
Moroccan	Saha wa'afiab	
Norwegian	Skål	"Sh-coal"
Occitan (France/Spain/Italy)	A la vòstra	
Pakistani	Sanda bashi	
Philippine	Mabuhay	
Polish	Na zdrowie	"Nose-DRAW-via"

Portuguese (Brazil)	Tim-tim / Saúde	"Team-team" / "Saw-OO-day"
Portuguese (Portugal)	Chim-chim / Saude	"Tchim-tchim" / "Saw-OO-day"
Quechua (Peru/Bolivia)	Napai-cuna	
Romanian	Noroc	"No-ROKE"
Russian	Vashe zdorovie/Mir i druzhba	"VAH-shiz De-ROW-via" / "Mir-eat-RUGE-bah"
Serbian	Zivjeli / U zdravlje	"Zheeva-LEE" / "Ooze-DRAW-vlee-ay"
Sesotho (South Africa)	Nqa	
Sinhala (Sri Lanka)	Jaya Vewa	"Juh-yuh Vay-wah"
Slovak	Na zdravie	"Nose-DRAW-via"
Slovenian	Na zdravje	"Nose-DRAW-via"
Spanish	Salud	"Saw-LOOT"
Swahili	Afya / Vifijo	"OFF-yo"/"Vee-FEE-joe"
Swedish	Skål	"Sh-coal"
Tagalog (Phillipines)	Mabuhay	"Ma-BOO-eye"
Taiwanese	Kam-poe	"Come-PWAY"
Thai	Chok-die / Sawasdi	
Turkish	Serefe	"Sheriff-AY"
Ukrainian	Na zdorov'ya	"Gnaws-doe-ROVE-ya"
Vietnamese	Chúc s_c kh_e, Vô	"Chuck-sequoia-YO"
Welsh	Iechyd da	"YECH-id-da"
Wolof (Gambia)	Jaraama	

*Where you see a "Ch," that's that guttural clearing-your-throat sound, versus the "Tch" as in the word "itch." "Zh" is like the sound in the middle of the word "vision." And pretty much any time you see an R, it should be rolled with the tongue as best you can—except for the German and Dutch R's that come more from the back of the mouth.

Index